MW00795709

# MONTE CARMELO
## An Italian-American Community in the Bronx

LIBRARY OF ANTHROPOLOGY

Editor: Anthony L. LaRuffa

Editorial Assistant: Phyllis Rafti

Advisory Board: Edward Bendix, Mary Ann Castle, Robert DiBennardo,
May Ebihara, Paul Grebinger, Bert Salwen, Joel S. Savishinsky,
Mario Zamora

*Additional volumes in preparation*

ISSN: 0141–1012

This book is part of a series. The publisher will accept continuation orders which may
be cancelled at any time and which provide for automatic billing and shipping of each
title in the series upon publication. Please write for details.

# MONTE CARMELO

## An Italian-American Community in the Bronx

By Anthony L. LaRuffa

*Herbert H. Lehman College of the
City University of New York*

GORDON AND BREACH SCIENCE PUBLISHERS
New York   London   Paris   Montreux   Tokyo   Melbourne

© 1988 by OPA (Amsterdam) B.V. All rights reserved. Published under license by Gordon and Breach Science Publishers S.A.

Gordon and Breach Science Publishers

Post Office Box 786
Cooper Station
New York, New York 10276
United States of America

Post Office Box 197
London WC2E 9PX
England

58, rue Lhomond
75005 Paris
France

Post Office Box 161
1820 Montreux 2
Switzerland

3–14–9 Okubo
Shinjuku-ku, Tokyo
Japan

Private Bag 8
Camberwell, Victoria 3124
Australia

Library of Congress Cataloging-in-Publication Data

LaRuffa, Anthony L., 1933–
  Monte Carmelo.

  (Library of anthropology; 9)
  Bibliography: p.
  Includes index.
    1. Italian Americans—New York (N.Y.)—Social
conditions.   2. Bronx (New York, N.Y.)—Social
conditions.   3. New York (N.Y.)—Social conditions.
I. Title.  II. Series.
F128.9.I8L37    1988        974.7'27500451       87–35520
ISBN 2–88124–253–7

No part of this book may be reproduced or utilized in any form or by any means, electronic or mechanical, including photocopying and recording, or by any information storage or retrieval system, without permission in writing from the publishers. Printed in the United States of America.

*In memory of my parents,*
*Angelina Aquilano LaRuffa (1892–1964) and*
*Francesco LaRuffa (1885–1971)*

# Contents

# Tables

# Introduction to the Series

One of the notable objectives of the *Library of Anthropology* is to provide a vehicle for the expression in print of new, controversial, and seemingly "unorthodox" theoretical, methodological, and philosophical approaches to anthropological data. Another objective follows from the multi-dimensional or holistic approach in anthropology which is the discipline's unique contribution toward understanding human behavior. The books in this series will deal with such fields as archaeology, physical anthropology, linguistics, ethnology, and social anthropology. Since no restrictions will be placed on the types of cultures included, a New York or New Delhi setting will be considered as relevant to anthropological theory and methods as the highlands of New Guinea.

The *Library* is designed for a wide audience and, whenever possible, technical terminology will be kept to a minimum. In some instances, however, a book may be unavoidably somewhat esoteric and consequently will appeal only to a small sector of the reading population — advanced undergraduate students in addition to professional social scientists.

My hopes for the readers are twofold: first, that they will enjoy learning about people; second, and perhaps more important, that they will come to experience a feeling of oneness with humankind.

*Anthony L. LaRuffa*

# Acknowledgments

My debt to the people of Monte Carmelo is inestimable. Living among them and being part of their lives exposed me to countless enriching experiences. There are so many individuals who deserve particular recognition but to respect their privacy I refer to them as a group. These Monte Carmelesi are, and will always be, very special to me. I cherish their friendship.

My *parenti* in general, and my siblings in particular, have been important sources of information on the Italian-American experience. Each of my siblings — Antoinette, Lena, Josephine, Joey, Rose, Marion, Louise, Angie, Catherine and Frances — deserve my gratitude, and I give it with love.

To another kin grouping, the Raftis, I am grateful for some of the background information on Monte Carmelo. Phyllis Rafti, in particular, was responsible for my initial visit to the community almost a decade ago. I can still recall that as we walked along one of the streets, she proudly pointed to the building in which her father was born. Just half a block away, the upper level of the Church of Our Lady of Mount Carmel was still under construction when her father was baptized in the basement part of the building.

My debt to Phyllis, who gave me constant support and encouragement, is immeasurable. Despite her own numerous professional and domestic responsibilities, she always managed to find the time to assist me with many phases of the fieldwork. In addition, she helped edit the manuscript, did most of the photography and prepared the index. Phyllis's critical reading of the manuscript provided me with many valuable suggestions. I will always be grateful for her devotion.

My children — Toni, Erik, and Gia — merit a note of appreciation because they were involved either directly or indirectly in my research. The oldest, Toni, visited me from time to time and listened patiently as her father talked incessantly about the community. At times, the two of us would join a group of Monte Carmelesi in a café for refreshments and conversation. My son, Erik, moved in with me a few months after I had rented an apartment in the community. He often shared with me his experiences in Monte Carmelo. Gia, my youngest child and Phyllis's daughter, frequently accompanied me to community events and enjoyed being part of the Italian-American enclave.

I wish to thank Dr. Mary Ann Castle for her critical appraisal of the manuscript. Her suggestions proved invaluable in the subsequent revisions of the text. Dr. Richard Gambino and Edyth Caro deserve a note of thanks for their substantive and editorial comments.

I am particulary grateful to Harriet Shabowsky for her patience and perseverence in typing the major portion of the manuscript. Thanks go to Monica Teran for typing several sections.

Much appreciation is owed to many of my students, a number of whom have since graduated from Lehman College. In various ways they shared with me their knowledge of the texture of Italian-American life in different neighborhoods of the Bronx. Some provided me with important contacts. Because quite a few of them are presently living in Monte Carmelo or have only recently moved from the community I cannot, unfortunately, acknowledge them by name. I can state, however, that through the years the bonds of friendship have linked us together.

Finally, I would like to express my gratitude to Herbert H. Lehman College of the City University of New York for awarding me a Faculty Fellowship Grant which enabled me to undertake full-time research in the community during part of the 1981–82 academic year.

# Introduction

There are somewhat fewer than 12,000,000 Italian-Americans of both single ancestry and multiple ancestry living in the United States. They comprise 5.3 percent of the total population. Most Italian-Americans are located in the Middle Atlantic states (New York, New Jersey, and Pennsylvania). There are also significant numbers in New England, the Midwest, and California, though they represent a smaller percentage of the total populations in their respective areas compared with the Mid-Atlantic region.

For more than a century, New York City and its environs have been the primary areas of settlement for a substantial number of the immigrants and their descendants. Approximately 18 percent of the Italian-American population of the country reside in an area encompassing New York City, Westchester County, Rockland County, Long Island (all in the lower part of New York State), and Bergen County (New Jersey). It is within this area that the original Monte Carmelesi settled and where their offspring and well over 2,000,000 other Italian-Americans live.

This is a study[1] of one particular segment of the larger metropolitan region. Located in the central part of the Bronx, Monte Carmelo's beginning as an Italian-American community dates back to the last decade of the nineteenth century when immigrants from southern Italy and Italian-Americans from neighborhoods in New York City began moving in. Over the next four decades, Monte Carmelo emerged as the prime Italian-American community of the Bronx where approximately 30,000 people inhabited an area of approximately about 100 square blocks. During the past twenty-five years the community has atrophied as thousands of Italian-Americans left Monte Carmelo for the more affluent neighborhoods of the Bronx, Queens, and suburbia where they often settled in with former Monte Carmelesi and with Italian-Americans who had come from other neighborhoods.

This study of Monte Carmelo provides a description of the historical background of the immigrants and a demographic, social, and cultural analysis of the enclavement process. Also included are

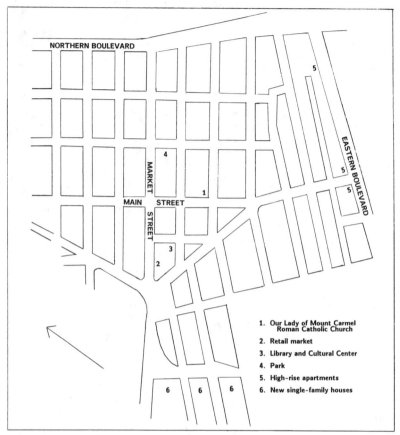

Figure 1. Monte Carmelo

data on community life today as it is manifested in different forms: in the perceptions and life history information of a number of the people; in some of the happenings; in family organization; and in the structure and role of community associations. Finally, certain misconceptions about the Monte Carmelesi and their community are presented and issues relating to Italian-Americans in general are explored.

Although the study of a particular community in a large metropolitan setting cannot furnish definitive answers to many of the questions that could be asked about Italian-American ethnicity, it does provide us with a clearer understanding of the larger population. This in turn generates the types of questions that help clarify the issues more precisely.

Two important issues that have received a considerable amount of attention in the social science literature are ethnicity and assimilation.[2] The study of Monte Carmelo, in part, addresses these issues, especially in terms of ethnicity as a process rather than a static phenomenon.

In viewing the Monte Carmelesi in the wider context, that is as part of a larger ethnic population, one finds that the intra-ethnic variations within the community itself are reflective of some of the variations occurring in the Italian-American population as a whole. At the same time there is an expression of unity in secular and religious celebrations, symbols of the collective identity not only of the community itself but of numerous segments of the Italian-American population in the metropolitan area.

The Italian-Americans as an ethnic population share a similar culture that includes language, values, beliefs, cuisine, recreational and aesthetic preferences, material items, and a common history. The latter may be broadly interpreted to mean the past life styles of the southern region of Italy. The regional society with its culture and subcultures provided the backdrop for the ethnic process in a new context. This process involves adaptations to changing circumstances resulting in variations within the ethnic population. Southern Italians constituted the primary component of the Italian-American population. The ethnic web extended further to incorporate other regional groups and their subcultures. A common history, therefore, can be viewed from different levels: subregions, including towns; regions; and, the Italian nation. A commonality of background is a crucial element in the identification of an ethnic population and is analogous to consanguineal ties in the formation of kinship groups.

The significance of societal bonds with other Italian-Americans — affinal membership in the kindred, fictive and ritual kin ties, spatial ties, friendship relationships, and membership in associations with coethnics — also provides an important perspective in the delineation of the ethnic population. It is this combination of cultural and societal criteria — in varying forms and in different quantities — that identify the Italian-American as a distinct population.

The essence of an ethnic population, and at the same time the manifold variations that exist within, are evident in Monte Carmelo. This is not to suggest that Monte Carmelo is representative of other Italian-American communities or that the Monte Carmelesi typify the 12,000,000 Italian-Americans living in the United States. Nor do they serve as a model for the more than 2,000,000 Italian-Americans inhabiting the New York metropolitan region. Although not precisely representative, Monte Carmelo shares a similar history and is characterized by the intra-ethnic social and cultural variations found in many Italian-American populations living in other urban and suburban communities of the United States. It is quite probable that in some neighborhoods there may be a higher distribution of certain variants and correspondingly a lower number of others. The Italian-Americans of Oceanside, Long Island display a different range of variation as compared with those residing in Monte Carmelo. Indeed, the hundreds of neighborhoods throughout the metropolitan region where Italian-Americans comprise a large component of the population evidence differences within the ethnic spectrum.

Besides demonstrating that significant intra-ethnic variations occur even with an ostensibly traditional Italian-American community, a study of Monte Carmelo also reveals that there exist important linkages between the community as a mecca of *Italianita* and Italian-Americans throughout the general region. As a symbol of Italianness, it transcends its spatial parameters and draws together a variety of Italian-American types who view it as the archetypical Italian-American community.

Finally, a social history and ethnographic study of Monte Carmelo and data on residential preferences of Italian-Americans in the metropolitan area compel us to seriously question the views of the class assimilationists who argue that as Italian-Americans move into the "mainstream" of American society the glow of ethnicity dims. It appears to me that something very different occurs. Italian-Americans as an ethnic population change, and as they change they display a resplendent array of varying colors embedded in a matrix of history, symbols, residence, and social ties.

## NOTES

1. The data and interpretations presented in this study are the result of four-and-a-half years of fieldwork in the community, beginning in January 1982. I have been a resident of Monte Carmelo since October 1983. The majority of names of people, places and organizations have been changed to ensure anonymity.
2. Some of the social scientists who have published on these issues include Alba (1985), Barth (1969), Castile and Kushner (1981), Crispino (1980), DeConde (1971), di Leonardo (1984), Gans (1982), Glazer and Moynihan (1975, 1983), Gordon (1964), Greeley (1974), Horowitz (1985), Keyes (1979), Lopreato (1970), Steinberg (1981), and Tomasi (1985).

Photographs

Above: Church of Our Lady of Mount Carmel. For more than eighty years, the church has been the principal representation of *Italianita* in the community.
Opposite *(Top)*: Handball courts in Market Street Park. The Italian and American flags symbolize Italian-American hegemony in Monte Carmelo.
*(Bottom)*: Typical private house. Home ownership has always been an important goal for Italian-Americans. Many of the proprietors of these older private homes are Italian-Americans.

Above: Typical apartment buildings. The relatively low rents have discouraged a number of Italian-Americans from moving out of the community.

Opposite *(Top)*: New single-family houses. Most of these homes have been purchased by Italian-Americans.

*(Bottom right)*: Monte Carmelo Branch Library and Cultural Center. Various community events are held at the Center.

*(Bottom left)*: High-rise apartment building. In more recent years, the construction of multi-apartment complexes, including low-income housing units, has contributed to the ethnic heterogeneity of the neighborhood.

Above: Church of Our Lady of Mount Carmel decorated for the Feast of St. Anthony. Opposite *(Top)*: People celebrating Italy's winning of the World Cup (July 1982). The soccer victory sparked an incredible display of joy and pride. *(Bottom)*: Feast of St. Anthony. In terms of time, money, and crowds, St. Anthony is the major festival in the community.

# CHAPTER ONE

# Historical Prologue, Part I: The Italian Background

Monte Carmelo, a relatively small segment of the northern-most borough of the largest urban center in the United States, has experienced a history which bears some commonality with other Italian-American communities within the same metropolis and in other cities of the United States. Many of these communities or ethnic enlaves emerged in the late 1800s and in the early twentieth century as immigrants left their towns and cities of southern Italy to begin new lives in the expanding cities of a new and strange land.[1]

Certainly, one of the most compelling and perplexing questions is: "Why did so many people travel so far for so little?" Various scholars, including Foerster (1965), Covello (1972), and others, focus on a wide variety of socio-cultural and physical factors to account for such an enormous outflow of southern Italians from their natal communities. Rather than view one particular factor as the primary reason for the exodus — although in any one specific instance a particular factor may have caused a person or a family to emigrate — it would be more helpful to consider a wide variety of interacting variables which provided the context for individual decisions.

If one had to define the general condition of life for the millions of Italians living in Calabria, Sicily, Campania, Basilicata, and Apulia, it could best be described by the phrase *la miseria*. *La miseria* is more than a state of mind; it is a way of life that has been shaped by historical, social, and physical forces.

Southern Italy had experienced more than two millenia of foreign rule — two thousand years of various forms of political and economic oppression. With the unification of Italy in 1870, there was little reason for rejoicing since, for many, life became more destitute. Pledges of land reform were merely empty promises. Land, the very basis of *contadini* (peasant) survival, grew increasingly more scarce as burdensome taxes forced many of the peasants to sell their land.

The land itself was certainly a mixed blessing. For the small landowners and the *jornalieri* (day laborers) who worked the lands of the *latifondisti* (estate owners), working the parched ground was a grueling task. The hot sun, the sparse rain, the dry winds that came north from the African deserts to destroy the maturing crops, and a soil that had been leached by winter rain all made for a very precarious existence. The desperate need for water was exploited by the *latifondisti* or their agents "who leased the privilege of its use usually to one person, who in turn sublet water privilege to small farmers able to produce some kind of guarantee for future payment" (Covello 1972: 41).

The estate owners were often absentee landlords who spent their time in the cities and delegated responsibilities to the *gabelotti* (land agents) who leased out the land for the *latifondo*. In time, the *gabelotto* became more of a speculator than land manager and, as such, acquired a considerable amount of power in the communities. He cheated the *latifondo* and doubly cheated the *contadino*. Not only did he lease land to the *contadino* at a considerable profit for himself, but charged exorbitant prices for seed and livestock. This type of exploitation fostered a constant state of indebtedness.

The *contadini* and the *jornalieri* and their families not only suffered the consequences of an exploitative agrarian system but were victims of harsh tax laws. Taxes were levied on land, dairy and draft animals, and on the family unit. The family was also required to give up its young men for military service. These tax laws and military conscription were associated with the new reunification government. It appears that the burdens were greater for the *contadini* and *jornalieri* after, rather than before, the reunification of Italy.

In addition to the economic and political factors mentioned above, there were other contributory reasons which moved millions of people to leave their homelands to seek out a new life in the United States. Natural calamities and diseases may have influenced one's decision. Malaria and cholera were two diseases which enervated many of the people. *La miseria* was further exacerbated by the periodic earthquakes, volcanic eruptions, and tidal waves which killed tens of thousands of people and destroyed entire communities.[2]

Furthermore, some individuals probably responded to the consequences of a depressed market for such agricultural exports as grapes and olives. The persuasiveness of a *padrone* (boss or middleman) with ties to shipping companies and employers of cheap labor in the United States might have convinced a particular individual or family to emigrate. Kinspeople and *paesani* (fellow townspeople) who had already left and had settled into ethnic neighborhoods springing up in a number of urban centers in the United States often tried to persuade others from their kindreds and towns to emigrate. In the early years of the mass exodus from southern Italy, which extended over a thirty-four year period (1880–1914), it was usually the men who left, returned, and then emigrated once again, in many cases with wife and offspring. During that era as well, there was a flow back and forth, with the greater number of men ultimately staying in the United States, where they were later joined by their wives and their children.

An overview of many of the contributing factors which created a general milieu within which any one person or group of persons made a specific decision to emigrate may overlook the specific dynamics of a particular situation. A number of recent immigrants to Monte Carmelo spoke about the better educational and employment opportunities that would be available, not necessarily for themselves, but for their children. Some parents made the decision to emigrate just prior to their son's eligibility for the draft. A man's dissatisfaction with his job prompted yet another person to emigrate. Strained interpersonal relationships with kinspeople and *paesani* probably reinforced a number of decisions which were ostensibly based on economic reasons. There were also those who were driven by the excitement of a new beginning. The old immigrants, however, those who were part of that great outpouring at the turn of the century, were truly the generation fleeing *la miseria*. Some settled in Monte Carmelo; others came to the community by way of East Harlem, the Lower East Side, and Morrisania.

Those settling in Monte Carmelo in the early years were some of the men, women, and children of the huge wave of Italian immigration. According to Robert Foerster (1969: 327), one of the foremost scholars of Italian immigration during the latter nineteenth century and early twentieth century, the number of Italian immigrants in the United States in 1890 was 182,580. Within the next decade, the Italian immigrant population increased by more than 250 percent (ibid.). During the first ten years of the twentieth century more than 2,104,000 Italians arrived in the United States, an average of 201,400 per year (ibid.). It was at this time that numerous Italian-American urban communities, Monte Carmelo included, began to develop. These ethnic neighborhoods were not only the product of direct migration from an Italian town or city; there was, in addition, a substantial inflow from other communities within the same U.S.

cities. It was this combination of external immigration and internal migration, especially intra-urban movements, that accounts for the growth of the various Italian-American urban neighborhoods in the United States.

A somewhat conservative estimate of the number of Italian immigrants in New York City at the turn of the twentieth century indicates that there were approximately 200,000 spread out in disproportionate numbers over the five boroughs (Mangano 1975: 3). There were 110,000 in Manhattan, 50,000–60,000 in Brooklyn, and 30,000 in the other three boroughs combined (ibid.). If one were to add the second generation population figure to that of the immigrant population, the total was in excess of 420,000 (ibid.:8).

Large numbers of these Italian immigrants settled on the Lower East Side of Manhattan and between 104th and 120th Streets (from 2nd Avenue to the East River) in upper Manhattan; Brooklyn settlements included the southern part of the borough and the Williamsburg section. In the Bronx, Monte Carmelo attracted a substantial number of Italian immigrants. These immigrants settling in the various communities of New York City came to work as shoemakers, barbers, operatives, ditch diggers, fruit vendors, grocers, stone cutters, masons, painters, ice and coal deliverers, rag collectors, contractors, plasterers, organ grinders, and artists. Some 80 percent were unskilled laborers and very few had more than three years of schooling.

If one were to follow a typical experience of this era, an experience that would include the general socio-cultural background and resources of the person or persons, the voyage, and the initial settlement, the scenario could be reconstructed in the following way.

One would begin with how the individual perceives himself/herself and the surrounding world. For the individual the world is seen primarily in terms of *la famiglia* (the family). The ties of blood are the ties that bind, and the closer the relationship, the stronger the bond. The individual is less ego-centered, but more a family person. One works in order to contribute to the maintenance of all family members. One's behavior is measured in terms of whether or not it shames or honors the family. Above all, it is imperative that there be a collective projection of *una bella figura* (a good image). A good image, however tenuous, is linked to two very important values in traditional Italian and Italian-American societies: honor and pride. These are intimately related to the worth or quality of the person as an individual but, more importantly, as a member of a family. Even poverty in its most brutal form has not been able to undermine the significance of honor and pride among Italians and Italian-Americans. It may well be that a long history of poverty could account for the strong emphasis on these values. Under such circumstances one takes pride in what one is, rather than what one has. Honor, then, becomes a matter of protecting one's worth. These responsibilities are shared by one's family in particular and one's *parente* (kindred) in general.

Three illustrations exemplify the significance of honor and pride. Two incidents involve someone whom I shall call Joey and the time frame is the mid- 1940s and early 1950s. As a young teenager, Joey often played in the streets of the Bedford-Stuyvesant section of Brooklyn. Many of the boys had fashioned wooden guns armed with rubberbands and capable of discharging square pieces of oil cloth. It wasn't unusual for small groups to form friend-and-foe skirmish lines and to fire the oil cloth pieces at one another. Occasionally, individual youngsters would square off against one another. Such was the case involving Joey and a friend who lived across the street. In the ensuing exchange of oil cloth "bullets," Joey had gotten the upper hand and his friend's father intervened, striking Joey on the face. Joey returned home with the left side of his face puffy and very red. The friend's father was confronted by a representative of Joey's family, verbally thrashed, and given a stern warning. Interestingly, it was one of Joey's older sisters who acted as the family representative. Joey's older brother was in the service and his father was not informed in order to avoid the probability of violence. Joey's friend's father apologized and the family was satisfied.

Some years later, when Joey was in his first year of college, he was approached by a gang of Italian-American youths while talking to a friend outside of his home. The gang leader asked some questions and then began to jostle Joey and his friend. Soon he became more agitated and more violent and his blows harder. When it appeared that neither Joey nor his friend could be drawn into a fight, he made overtures of conciliation and left. Somehow word of the incident had gotten to two of Joey's nephews. Armed with street weapons — socks loaded with rocks — they sought out the gang leader and made it very clear to him that he was never to physically or verbally abuse their uncle again. Not long after, the gang leader profusely apologized to Joey, claiming that he was not aware of who Joey was. The matter had been settled quietly and quickly through family intervention. In this particular case, a modest amount of violence was used.

A recent incident which occurred in Monte Carmelo further illustrates the importance of honor and pride to a family who had immigrated from a town near Naples to the United States in 1970. As first-generation Italian-Americans they see themselves more as Italian than American and, consequently, their perceptions of proper behavior vary from that of their more American-oriented co-ethnics. The Romanos occupy the first two floors of a two-family house and rent the top floor to a man and his seventeen-year-old son Matthew. The latter invited a group of his friends, males and females, to visit him. At first they were sitting on the outside steps which lead to the second floor. Mr. Romano suggested that the group sit on the bench and chairs which were situated outside the first floor entrance and could be easily viewed from inside. At one point one of the girls sat on Matthew's lap. Mr. Romano immediately came out and told Matthew that this was not permissible. Although Matthew and Mr. Romano are not related, Matthew's behavior reflected on both the landlord and his family. His nineteen-year-old daughter often sits outside with her female friends and cousins, both male and female. A public display of male-female intimacy, though engaged in by nonrelatives, may suggest that his daughter could also do such things and, if she did, it would be a flagrant sign of disrespect toward her parents and would bring shame and dishonor to her family. Mr. and Mrs. Romano are proud of their daughter Anna. She only goes out to work, or occasionally with female friends and relatives. When she does go out, she must be home by midnight and her mother stays awake and reprimands her if she is not. Young Anna has been socialized to express those female qualities which are highly valued in traditional Italian society: purity, modesty, and submissiveness. All of this was compromised by Matthew's behavior outside of Mr. Romano's house, and Mr. Romano insisted that appropriate steps be taken to reestablish *la bella figura*.

Covello (1972) and Maraspino (1968) report on the vendetta and crimes of honor in southern Italy as violent ways of redressing family grievances. Furthermore, there are instances in which the parties seek out an influential person who then attempts to work out a solution where both families can save face. There is also the issue of intra-familial honor and pride as manifested in the behavioral patterns and role relationships of the various members. One often hears from informants how important respect is since respect nourishes honor. An informant who immigrated from Calabria stated that when she was a child she and her older sister would kiss the right hand of their parents and seek their blessings before going to bed. After the family had settled in New York the practice was discontinued; though for years after the father would, from time to time, request, and even insist, that the children kiss his hand. Apparently he was particularly sensitive to the growing lack of respect which he perceived.

Parents expect their children to be obedient. Disobedience is viewed as a lack of respect. Daughters especially must obey their parents, and it is expected that as long as they live in their parents' household they must observe parental rules. To do otherwise would be an egregious act of disrespect.

What was life like for a southern Italian girl living in a relatively typical Italian town? Despite the changes that might have occurred between 1910 and 1950 for example, young women growing up in these two different time periods were probably more alike in their attitudes, values and, to some extent, behavioral patterns, than they were different. Unlike boys, girls were expected to assume "useful work" at an early age. By the age of six and seven they were under the strict supervision of their mothers and their brothers. The mother, of course, was the most important role model and the primary teacher in preparing the girl for her future roles as wife and mother. Although the young girl was expected to help in the fields, her main responsibilities revolved around the home. She looked after the younger children, did some of the housekeeping, attended to the fire and water supply and, in general, became a mother surrogate. In addition she was expected to sew, embroider, spin, and weave (Covello 1972: 196). "The only relaxation and diversion," writes Covello (ibid.: 197–198), "was offered by church attendance on Sundays, family festivals, and formal visits to or by some relatives of the family. [The] chastity of the girl was the main factor that determined her moral status" (ibid.: 198). The mother and sons were especially involved in the supervision of the daughter's behavior and were more concerned than the father about the daughter becoming *sistemate*, that is, married to someone who could provide for her and their children. Landowners, merchants, and artisans were desirable spouses; sheperds and day laborers were considered less acceptable. A woman with a substantial dowry was more likely to marry well, but such a case was rare. Most families were too impoverished to provide more than a basic trousseau, the end product of long hours of embroidery and crocheting. These items symbolized three basic areas of domestic life: the bridal clothing represented the new role that the woman undertook in the household; the bed linen signified the importance of children; and embroidered kitchen placemats, though rarely used, symbolized the hoped for *abbondanza* (plentifulness). This was the sort of life that a mother and father expected for their daughter and the daughter expected for herself. Often the parents played a major role in selecting a husband for their daughter. In general then, a female's life was confined primarily to the domestic sphere and she occupied a subservient position in relation to the male members of her natal and conjugal households.

Boys, no less than girls, were constrained by the exigencies of familial survival. Like the girls, boys rarely received more than three years of formal education. Although at a somewhat later age than girls, boys also assumed responsibilities at a fairly early age. Before the age of ten, many of them became craftsmen's apprentices. Others became shepherds or were given custodial care over whatever few farm animals the family either possessed or had contracted to look after. Traditionally, males were expected to develop a particular style or role pattern which was somewhat obverse to that of females. If females were primarily concerned with the private sector, males were more involved with public aspect of life. Males in Italian society "hung out" in groupings based on kin ties — both consanguineal and ritual — and friendship. These groups met in cafés, played cards together, or gathered in or near certain commercial establishments. On Sundays, especially, many of the men would dress up and meet their friends, cousins, and *compari* in one of the local cafés. Their wives, mothers, daughters, and sisters would be attending mass.

The innocence of the female was seemingly balanced by the worldliness of the male. It was expected, for example, that the male as husband would be the experienced sexual partner. "The repression of [the] sex drive," writes Covello (ibid.: 199), "was more lax where men were concerned. Government supervised prostitution was practiced in every larger community, and the patronizing of the local *bordelli* by young men was not considered as offensive behavior." Despite their eagerness to demonstrate an image of virility, men were very careful about whom they courted and married. There were women to "play with" and there was the woman who had been properly socialized to assume the role of wife and mother. The man expected such a woman to be obedient, loyal, thrifty, knowledgeable about household responsibilities, a virgin before marriage, and fertile after marriage. To him marriage was more of a practical arrangement than an emotional relationship. As a partner in a marital relationship, he was expected to work hard to support his family and to maintain the respect of the community.

For both men and women role responsibilities were clearly delineated, especially those activities revolving around the home. Women were the caretakers, and men and children the care receivers. Not only did husbands and fathers expect this of their wives and daughters, but the sons in the family expected this of their mothers and sisters. If there was any crossing of role lines, it was more likely that the woman would help out in the fields or work in the family store. Men, on the other hand, were less likely to undertake household tasks that were traditionally performed by women.

As stated above, the individual's perception of the world was primarily shaped by the relationships and role learning experienced within the context of *la famiglia*. The broader framework of the kindred included aunts, uncles, cousins, grandparents, *comari* (godmothers), *compari* (godfathers), and affines, all of whom were significant for the individual, providing an extensive network of supportive relatives — a network which became especially helpful for those who immigrated to Monte Carmelo and to other similar Italian communities in the United States.

Beyond the individual's *parenti* (relatives), the world consisted of *amici*, one's friends. Very often *amici* were also *parenti* or individuals drawn into the kindred through formal ritual ties, i.e., the *comparaggio*, or simply through an informal *comara* or *compare* relationship. These were usually individuals of the same sex. Once an individual was involved in a serious *amicizia* (friendship) relationship, the obligations which each had to the other were unequivocal. Loyalty was perhaps the most conspicuous obligation of a friendship association. Loyalty to a friend was merely an extension of fidelity to one's family. Like family, friends were called upon to use their contacts to help a person secure a position, to circumvent a bureaucratic snag, or to assist a person repair a house. A friend was also someone you enjoyed playing cards with and drinking wine or liqueurs with at a café. A friend was a person with whom you shared the tragic loss of a young child who succumbed to dysentery, cholera, or typhoid fever.

As the individual's world widened beyond *parenti* and *amici*, one encountered *vicini* (neighbors) and *paesani*, who were the co-inhabitants of a spatially meaningful unit, the town. The town as a socio-political entity comprised an institutional nexus of church and state and a socio-economic hierarchy. Lopreato (1970: 24–25), referring to the study of Leopoldo Franchetti on social conditions in Basilicata and Calabria at about the time of national unification, lists

three main classes of people: a small number of very powerful landlords; a group of lawyers too numerous for the needs of a land with very little industry and commerce; and a vast mass of landless peasants living in economic depression and semi-slavery. Very few were the peasants who owned a piece of land, and still fewer were the entrepreneurs, the artisans, and the intelligentsia capable of influencing socio-economic conditions.

From a political perspective it was primarily a two-tier stratum system: a landed gentry which either directly or indirectly controlled the political life of the town, and all the others who had little or no access to the reigns of power.

The church, perhaps more so than any other institution, symbolized the essence of town life. For centuries most individuals lived out their entire lives within the sounds of the church or churches' bells. The life cycle, i.e., birth (baptism), childhood (first communion), puberty (confirmation), marriage, and death were marked by church rituals. Despite the cynicism and anticlericalism engendered by a long history of exploitation of the peasantry by the church, first as a large land owner and then as a social and political ally of the landed gentry, the people in general still felt a strong allegiance towards it. One might have criticized the behavior of a particular priest, but one would have never questioned the importance of a marriage or mortuary ritual. Not to baptize an infant was virtually unthinkable.

Women were the active churchgoers, although men continued to maintain important ritual ties. Daily and weekly attendance at mass and novenas were part of the female role and, as such, further reinforced male-female role differences. The church was an extension of the home for a woman. She continued to care for her children, husband, and other kinspeople through prayers, the lighting of candles, and vows made to particular saints and the Madonna. It was usually the woman who would touch the statue of a saint or Madonna and reverently kiss her hands as a sign of devotion and affection.

The saints and the Madonna played an important part in the religious life of the people. Dealing with saints was very pragmatic since they had special powers to resolve specific problems. Saint Anne was prayed to by pregnant women who were anxious to have a normal birthing experience and a healthy infant. Young women concerned with fulfilling the role expectations of their society, i.e., wife and mother, sought the assistance of San Nicola or San Giovanni. San Antonio, San Gennaro, and San Francesco d'Assisi also were saints popular throughout southern Italy.

The Madonna, like the saints, received a considerable amount of attention. In many homes one would have found statues of the Madonna with candles burning as offerings for favors received or requests made. Although the Virgin Mary was a specific religious figure, her manifestations reflected local traditions and histories. The Madonna de Monte Verde was popular in the Abruzzi region; the Black Madonna, La Madonna di Seminara from Calabria; La Madonna de Loreto from Sicily; and La Madonna di Monte Carmelo from Campania were some of the more famous representations of the Virgin Mary.

The emphasis on the Madonna and the saints as well as the numerous supernatural beliefs and practices including, among others, a fear of the consequences of *mal occhio* (the evil eye) or of a bewitching spell comprised the folk component of southern Italian religious life. The precariousness of life, a high infant mortality rate, and the anxieties generated by role pressures were just some of the reasons why people were particularly sensitive to the potential hazards of the evil eye or the possible negative consequences of someone's *invidia* (envy). Infants and young children were especially susceptible and had to be protected with the appropriate amulets and scapulas. Those who became afflicted were prayed over and anointed with oil, and folk specialists who were especially adept in dealing with the problem were consulted. These folk specialists were often women who had "inherited" their powers from their mothers.

Town life, which the individual shared with *vicini* and *paesani*, was also characterized by festivites associated with the patron saint or the special Madonna. These activities included both a religious aspect — involving a mass in honor of the town patron and a procession through the streets in which the statue of the patron was borne by the townsmen — and a secular component. The secularity of the *festa* (feast) was manifested in music, special foods, and fire works and frequently attracted people from nearby communities.

*Feste* were often opportunities for communities to compete with one another.[3]

The individual's more meaningful world, therefore, consisted of social relationships that were shared with *familigia, parenti, vicini,* and *paesani.* These relationships were expressed in a context of values, attitudes, beliefs, and rituals. The individual's world in general, however, was ultimately shaped by economic, social, and political forces which transcended the boundaries of neighborhood, town, or province. Yet the larger world and its representatives, whether government officials or simply a person who might have stopped off for a brief visit, were viewed with suspicion and with some degree of trepidation. *Stranieri* (outsiders), as they were called, were those who did not belong; *stranieri* were those who could cause problems. Southern Italians have had more than two millennia of experience with various forms of external economic and political domination and, consequently, an acute sensitivity to all *stranieri* as symbols of domination became part of their mode of adaptation. The *stranieri* in the piazzi and streets of Nicotera, Muro Lucano, Ostuni, or Anzi were no less viewed as individuals who might create problems and disrupt the routine of community life than were the *stranieri* who moved into such Italian-American neighborhoods as Monte Carmelo in more recent times. However, the perception of *stranieri* has changed, reflecting the prejudices of U.S. society. This will be discussed in the next chapter.

There was for the individual yet another level of awareness which extended even beyond the category of *stranieri:* this was *cristiani.* Although initially one might view this category as consisting of all those who were baptized as Christians — which an Italian would interpret to be Catholic — the emphasis was less on religious identification and more on one's identity with the "human family." To leave the familiar setting of *parenti* and community, to travel to a strange city, to embark on a voyage of thousands of miles across an often stormy ocean with little or no money, to transcend a world of common experiences with little or no understanding of what awaits them — all of this the southern Italians endured with the hope that the people they would encounter, if not *parenti* or *paesani,* or even *stranieri* from other towns and other provinces, would at least be *cristiani.*

This is what Angelina was hoping and praying for when she and her two daughters began the long journey from Polistena in Calabria to Naples, where they boarded the ocean-going ship for the voyage to New York. Her husband, Francesco, had left for the United States in 1913 and before he had earned sufficient money to send for his family, war erupted in Europe. Now, seven years later, his wife and two daughters were to join him.

For little Antoinette, her sister Pasqualina, and their mother Angelina, the sea voyage was an extremely frightening and uncomfortable experience. As steerage passengers, they were exposed to dreadful sanitary conditions and to the humiliation of cramped quarters. The two children often refused to eat because of the nausea brought on by the rough seas and stormy weather. In order to induce them to eat, Angelina would buy food from the steerage peddlers who would sell items which were more representative of the preferences of the passengers.

The stormy weather persisted and Angelina was frightened that the ship would sink and all would perish. She often prayed and read her prayer book, beseeching the Madonna to bring them safely through the storm. The two children had scapulas of the Madonna pinned on their undershirts to insure them a safe voyage. With each passing day Angelina grew more apprehensive about the prospect of surviving the trip. She had not seen her husband for seven years and her youngest daughter, Pasqualina, was born a few months after Francesco had left for the United States. It would have been a cruel twist of fate if young Pasqualina and her father were never to see each other.

The long days and nights of rough seas finally ended, and not long thereafter Angelina and her daughters were standing on a long line in a huge room — the Great Hall on Ellis Island — where millions of immigrants were examined for physical, mental or moral "defects." Those who were judged unfit were shipped back. Angelina, Antoinette, and Pasqualina looked fit enough to pass muster, and so they were permitted to enter a strange country: three bewildered, weary, and timid people searching for some kind of link with this strange new world. They saw people waving and others hugging and kissing. Angelina looked hard for the face she had not seen for seven years. Neither of her two children would recognize it; Antoinette was two years old and Pasqualina was in her mother's womb when their father left for New York. The thought of not finding her husband struck terror in the heart of Angelina. But Francesco was there and, as always on special occasions, he was impeccably dressed in a blue suit, white shirt, and dark tie. He had been to his barber friend that morning for a haircut, shave, and moustache trim. With him was his older brother Antonio, a shoemaker, who was living in a two-family home in Brooklyn that his family shared with his wife's sister's family. The children were hugged and kissed and fussed over. Angelina, as was expected, received a much more restrained greeting. But, for the moment, she was happy. The horrible voyage was over; the glaring eyes of the immigration inspectors were no longer threatening and, above all, she was with *parenti*.

She and her family stayed with her husband's brother's family for a short time and then moved to a rented house. In her new neighborhood, she found some comfort in knowing that people from her husband's town were living there. She had spent seven years in Polistena and had become familiar with the local life-styles. The family settled into the community, grew, and continued the odyssey of migration.

Others came, leaving their homes in Apulia, Campania, Basilicata, Calabria, and Sicily. There were those like Francesco, Angelina, and their young children who immigrated during the early decades of the twentieth century and settled in various Italian-American enclaves in New York City and Long Island, often moving from one Italian-American neighborhood to another. Pasquale Fusco and his family, for example, left their town of Avigliano and originally settled in lower Manhattan. Within a few years the family moved to Morrisania in the Bronx and then rented an apartment in Monte Carmelo. Some moved from Brooklyn to Monte Caremelo; some had lived in East Harlem for a few years before moving to Monte Carmelo. Meanwhile, a number of Italian-American families moved out of Monte Carmelo to other communities in the Bronx, Queens, Long Island, and Westchester and Rockland Counties.

Post-World War II Italian immigration, intra-city, and city to suburbia migration continued to affect the population of Monte Carmelo. Despite the inflow and outflow of people, the ethnic composition of the population remained predominantly Italian-American. During the past twenty-five years, however, Monte Carmelo has experienced significant demographic changes: what was a fairly extensive Italian-American community has become an Italian-American enclave in a multi-ethnic neighborhood.

## NOTES

1. Since the largest percentage of immigrants who first settled or ultimately settled in Monte Carmelo are from the southern provinces of Italy, the discussion that follows will be limited to that part of Italy.
2. Just a few years ago a destructive earthquake in the province of Campania killed thousands and left many homeless. Some of the victims emigrated to Monte Carmelo.
3. In more recent times the soccer field has become a major arena for competition between towns.

# CHAPTER TWO

# Historical Prologue, Part II:
# The Development of an Italian-American Enclave
# in the Bronx

Monte Carmelo, like so many other Italian-American urban neighborhoods in the Northeast, Midwest, and Far West of the United States, emerged as an ethnic community in the early years of this century. One observer (Cook 1913: 146) at the time noted that a number of the more affluent Italian-Americans who originally settled on the Lower East Side of Manhattan were attracted to the bucolic setting of what was referred to in former times as Fordham Manor, an area in the central part of the Bronx. The specific village of Monte Carmelo was located on land that formally belonged to the prominent Lorillard family. During the 1880s and 1890s, Irish and Germans moved into the "village," the Irish to work on the big estates and the Germans to establish their own truck farms. Subsequently, the Irish moved to other parts of the Fordham area and Italians began settling in Monte Carmelo.

Some of the Italians who moved in were laborers who helped build the railways, reservoirs, and streets of the Bronx. Many of these were immigrants from Sicily, Calabria, and Campania who were quite happy to find jobs and homes. The latter were more often than not the frame houses vacated by the Irish. The more affluent population of Italian-Americans who had fled from the oppressive slum conditions of lower Manhattan were quick to invest in real estate projects, including the construction of apartment buildings (Cook 1913: 146). From the early years of Italian settlement in Monte Carmelo we find a clear distinction between a relatively impoverished population of Italian immigrants working for low wages and a group of fairly prosperous Italian-Americans earning comfortable livings in their real estate enterprises. In just a short time an extensive ethnic network, within New York City and between Monte Carmelo and communities in Italy, was established.

Among the masses of Italians who had immigrated to the United States during the first decade of the twentieth century, there were those who sought out *parenti* and *paesani* in the growing Italian-American community of Monte Carmelo. They settled in an area which was subsequently to encompass approximately 100 square blocks.

By 1910, Italians as a foreign population constituted the third largest group in the general area (U.S. Bureau of the Census: 1913). However, in terms of the ethnic-spatial relationship factor, Italians made up the major proportion of the foreign population in the specific neighborhood of Monte Carmelo. As a result of the increasing inflow of Italians and Italian-Americans, the Catholic Church opened a storefront mission on Main Street in June of 1906 (*Golden Jubilee of Our Lady of Mount Carmel, 1906–1956* 1956: n.p.). In just over a year a new basement church, Our Lady of Mount Carmel, was completed (ibid.). Church records show that in a six year period more than 1,600 children were baptized. This is yet another indication of a rapidly expanding Italian-American community (ibid.). Within ten years, the entire church was constructed and the opening was celebrated by a parade which included thousands of children. One of the prominent families in the community presented the pastor with a statue of Our Lady of Mount Carmel which had been imported from Italy. The statue is still conspicuously displayed in the church and, along with St. Anthony, continues to play an important role in the ritual life of the community.

By 1930, Monte Carmelo had become a well-established Italian-American community with a large Italian-born population and a sizeable second generation which would soon begin producing offspring. More than 27,500 Italian-Americans resided in Monte Carmelo in 1930 (U.S. Bureau of the Census: 1931).[1]

The population remained relatively stable during the next ten years, wih a gain of slightly more than 500. The 1950 figures indicate a population decline of about 1,400. Beginning in the late forties and early fifties and continuing into the eighties, we are able to discern a population loss that becomes especially significant during the seventies. This decline in the number of Italian-Americans in Monte Carmelo continued for more than thirty years, although the rise in immigration from Italy during the late fifties and continuing into the early seventies was modest, and despite the fact that Italian-Americans were moving into Monte Carmelo from such neighborhoods as Morrisania and East Harlem, both of which were heavily populated Italian-American communities. This post-World War II outflow from Monte Carmelo can be partially attributed to the lure of the suburbs which were becoming more attractive because of the relatively inexpensive homes and the low-interest mortgages for the ex-serviceman. Also, some began to think of upward mobility in terms of such Bronx neighborhoods as Pelham Bay, Williamsbridge, Throgs Neck, Baychester, Country Club, and Morris Park. These are areas that continue to have high percentages of Italian-Americans, many of whom maintain ties with relatives, friends, the church, and the merchants in Monte Carmelo.

By 1960, there were 3,500 fewer Italian-Americans living in Monte Carmelo as compared with 1950 (U.S. Bureau of the Census: 1952). Again, the perception that home ownership is a sign of upward mobility caused a number of Italian-Americans to leave Monte Carmelo. Many had lived in apartment dwellings and few were interested in buying the older, wooden frame houses which were available in the neighborhood. Even today some of the young men and women living in the community state that staying in Monte Carmelo is an indication "that one is going nowhere." A number of young women commented that they want to escape the pressure of being constantly scrutinized by relatives and neighbors. "People know your business or want to know your business," is what they often say. To some extent this many have been the thinking of some of the younger people who usually moved out after they married. Very few young people left their homes or their neighborhood before marriage since unmarried offspring of any age were expected to live in the household of their parents.

People today frequently say that they wish to move out of Monte Carmelo because "the neighborhood is going bad." Let us examine what has occurred in the past twenty-five years to cause the Monte Carmelesi to perceive the community this way. By 1960, more than eight hundred Puerto Ricans had moved into Monte Carmelo. Within ten years the number had grown to over 5,300. At about the same time there was a substantial rise in the Black population and a significant decline in the Italian-American population to 21,500.

Some of the most violent ethnic confrontations in the history of Monte Carmelo took place during the late sixties.[2] Young Italian-American men and young Puerto Rican and Black men fought bloody battles on the streets of Monte Carmelo which often resulted in serious injuries and death. South Street became an active war zone and served as the boundary separating the Italian-American community from the expanding Puerto Rican and Black community. The youths formed battle lines on their respective sides of South Street and if the police failed to arrive on time, which was often the case, the war would continue. Frequently the battles spilled over to the grounds of the local high school where ethnic confrontations became commonplace. The most dramatic of these confrontations occurred when the New York City Transit Authority decided to inaugurate a new bus route along Main Street in the hope, perhaps, of assuring the safety of Puerto Rican and Black students attending North Steet High School. The reaction was violent: several buses were badly damaged and one was completely destroyed; a number of the students were seriously injured; and one Black youth was killed. This violence was not simply the senseless action of a group of Italian-Americans youths and, in some instances, older men. It was, in addition, a reflection of a mood and an attitude which a segment of the community shared. These confrontations and the ensuing violence were the efforts of some of the Monte Carmelesi to keep their neighborhood Italian-American or, at the very least, White. Actually the violence had the opposite effect — it hastened the exodus of Italian-Americans from Monte Carmelo.

Yet immigrants from Italy, Yugoslavia, and Albania continued settling in the community during the 1970s. The Yugoslavians and Albanians have had little difficulty integrating into the Italian-American dominated neighborhood. Many of the Albanians speak Italian and both groups are viewed as White and consequently are more like one's *parenti* and *paesani*. Blacks and Puerto Ricans have emerged as the threatening *stranieri* for the Monte Carmelesi. Over the years the Italian-Americans have become more Americanized in their perceptions of differences based on selected biological and socio-cultural characteristics, which our society associates with specific populations. In most instances these differences are perceived as menacing.

Population figures for 1980 clearly indicate a large outflow of Italian-Americans from Monte Carmelo. The total population of the community dropped to approximately 23,300 people (U.S. Bureau of the Census: 1982). Puerto Ricans numbered 8,800, an increase of more than 60 percent over a ten year period. Blacks accounted for 4,500 of the total. Puerto Ricans and Blacks together comprised more than 50 percent of the population of Monte Carmelo by 1980. The 1980 figures also indicate that the Puerto Rican population in the five census tracts which constitute the traditional "village" of Monte Carmelo was approximately 20 percent larger than the Italian-American population. Numbering 7,420, the Italian-Americans amounted to barely 32 percent of the 1980 population of the community. Of the approximately 1,600 remaining residents, the majority were Albanians and Yugoslavians.

The population figures clearly demonstrate that there has been a very substantial decline in the number of Italian-Americns living in Monte Carmelo over a thirty-year period (1950–1980). What is particularly intersting is that the exodus began about a decade before any discernible numbers of Puerto Ricans and Blacks began moving into the community. However, from 1960 to 1980, the Italian-American flight became substantial. In the thirty-year period between 1950 and 1980, 68 percent of the Italian-American population left Monte Carmelo. What had been an Italian-American community in terms of spatial distribution and ethnic homogeneity has become an Italian-American enclave within a multi-ethnic setting.

It is important to distinguish between two broad variants within the Italian-American population of Monte Carmelo. There are obviously more than two types in this particular Italian-American enclave or in the Italian-American population as a whole. Nevertheless, the two types provide distinct reference points from which the range of intra-ethnic variations can be more clearly delineated. The two types are distinguishable on the basis of orientation: the Italian-oriented individual represents one end of the spectrum and the American-oriented individual, the other.

Among the Italian-oriented type, Italian is the primary language spoken in the home, with other relatives, and with friends and neighbors. Even the language spoken reflects, in this specific cultural dimension, variations in the Italian-American spectrum. There are those who speak and understand only Italian; others, who speak Italian, speak and understand very little English; some speak very little Italian but understand a great deal of it; and there are many who combine English and Italian when conversing. Other variations exist as well. Perhaps the most American-oriented individual in the area of language usage is the person who responds negatively to Italian being used in conversation or commercial transactions. These are individuals who more often than not reject the "Italian" label and insist that they are Americans desipite the fact that there is a considerable amount of ambiguity about their own ethnic identity. Often these same individuals state that they are Americans whose ancestors emigrated from Italy.

In addition to communicating primarily and, in some instances, exclusively in Italian, the Italian-oriented type man would be more likely to hang out in cafés and join hometown associations. The woman, on the other hand, rarely "hangs out" except in the environs of the home; and a younger women's behavior is often subjected to the scrutiny of *parenti* and neighbors.

The cuisine of the Italian-oriented type consists of items such as a wide variety of pasta dishes, including a combination of pasta with such things as lentils, chick peas, and beans; escarole, broccoli, and other greens are thought to be especially salutary. Poultry, veal, lamb, and pork are consumed in the Italian-oriented households along with fresh fish and dried and salted cod and hake (*baccala* and *stoccafisso*). Bread, of course, is a major component of the meal and comes in a variety of shapes and designs. Certain feast days are often marked by very special bread designs. Other favorite victuals include cheeses, eggplants, tomatoes, fruits, artichokes, nuts, olives, and peppers.

Wine, frequently homemade, is drunk with meals in its pure form or diluted with water (*vinello*) or soda. Espresso is the preferred coffee not only as an after meal beverage, but throughout the day. Cordials[3] and espresso are the more typical refreshments for those who frequent the cafés.

The Italian-oriented person is more likely to attend mass conducted in Italian and to participate in the processions in honor of Our Lady of Mount Carmel, Saint Anthony, and the Madonna L'Addolorata (Our Lady of Sorrows). Such a person often reads *Il Progresso*, watches Italian programs on television, and listens to Italian radio stations. Recordings of famous Italian singers are as popular among the Italian-oriented segment of the population as are the Frank Sinatra records for the middle-aged American-oriented group. Also, the Italian-oriented person is more likely to visit Italy and to be visited by relatives from Italy. Phone calls between the Italian-oriented Monte Carmelesi and their *parenti* in Italy are commonplace.

These socio-cultural characteristics, as well as others, are expressive of the more Italian-like quality of Monte Carmelo, the "Little Italy" of the Bronx. This is the image that the *New York Times*, the *New York Daily News*, and other newspapers and magazines portray in their feature stories on ethnic neighborhoods. Recently, Monte Carmelo has been receiving a considerable amount of press coverage since it was cited as one of the safest neighborhoods in the country. This media exposure, focusing on the Italian quality of the enclave, has had a significant impact on the public's perception of Monte Carmelo.

The American-oriented type receives little or no publicity. Such an individual represents a group of people that has a longer history in Monte Carmelo and shares certain socio-cultural characteristics which distinguish them from their more Italian-oriented co-ethnics. For this sector of the population English is the primary language both within the home and among friends. A mixed peer group membership is much more common compared with the Italian-oriented type. Usually this group "hangs out" in front of certain stores and in the Market Steet park. During the period of confrontations and inter-ethnic violence, the park became one of the symbols of Italian-American homogeneity in the community. *Stranieri*, that is the Blacks and Puerto Ricans, were not allowed in the park. Even youngsters who had recently immigrated from Italy avoided using the facilities in the park because of the possibility of being intimidated by their more American-oriented co-ethnics.

A number of the older American-oriented men frequent certain eating places and play cards in private clubs. The older men, like their Italian-oriented counterparts, are part of all male groupings.

Young American-oriented women do not have the same restraints in interacting with male friends as their Italian-oriented age-mates do. For an older American-oriented woman, gender identification and similar role patterns make hanging out with other woman preferable. It is not unusual, however, for older men and women of both types to sit together outside their homes or apartment buildings for a few hours during the warmer days and evenings.

A number of the American-oriented category are high school drop-outs and few attend college. Many of the younger men play softball, football, and basketball. (Soccer is a favorite sport of the Italian-oriented type.) For the older American-oriented men, stickball and touch football games were major sports events played out in the streets of Monte Carmelo. Not only were these activities recreational but, in addition, opportunities for the participants to make some money. Even today many of the older American-oriented men follow the various sports' events, including football, baseball, boxing, and horse racing, and often bet on the outcome. Gambling is an important revenue producing activity in the enclave and the gambling network and racketeering in general is controlled by the American-oriented type.[4] I have been told that a very influential racketeer, a person who is more American than Italian, moved out of the community some time ago but returns to the neighborhood to "take care of business." There are large numbers of American-oriented individuals, like the racketeer, who were born and raised in Monte Carmelo, moved away, but return to "take care of business." These are the proprietors of bakeries, pork stores, liquor stores, hardware stores, and other businesses. There are also those who make the daily trip to the neighborhood to assume positions of leadership in various community organizations.

In addition to the characteristic features which distinguish the two general categories of Italian-oriented and American-oriented, the individuals themselves often view themselves as different. Mr. Romano and his wife, Rosa, for example, identify themselves as Italian. He, his wife, and three young daughters left their town in Campania for the United States fifteen years ago. Other than his daily commute to work at a cookie-producing plant in the Bronx and an occasional visit to his married daughter's home in New Jersey, Michele rarely leaves Monte Carmelo. His mother, two siblings, and numerous nieces and nephews live in the neighborhood. His oldest daughter and her family occupied the top floor of his two-family house until 1983. They since have returned to Michele's natal town.

Michele converses only in Italian and understands very little English. Rosa has some understanding of English but speaks Italian. Their youngest daughter is fluent in both English and Italian. In terms of cuisine, interpersonal relationships, role patterns and expectations, and ties with *parenti* and *paesani* in Italy, Michele's and Rosa's life style is quite compatible with their perceptions of themselves as Italian.

There are others like Michele and Rosa who view themselves as Italian. In a discussion with a number of Italian-American men and women who ranged in age from the late teens to the late thirties, two young women made it quite clear to the rest of us that they were Italians rather than Italian-Americans. They viewed others in the group as "Americans and not Italians." For them, language was the primary criterion for ethnic identification and maintaining ties with Italy was also important. Another woman argued that Italian ancestry should be the basis for ethnic identification. A twenty-year-old man stated that he viewed himself as an Italian-American and, as such, shared characteristics of the two cultures. In many ways the members of the group represented the variations that one encounters in the Italian-American spectrum, a spectrum which encompasses shades of ethnicity. The Monte Carmelesi express in their lifestyles and self-perceptions variations of a broad range of types which together comprise an Italian-American population living in what has become an ethnic enclave.

Having noted some of the socio cultural variations within the Italian-American population of Monte Carmelo, I will briefly consider a few of the more salient structural or organizational componets of the enclave.[5] One of the more visible organizations in the neighborhood is the Merchants Association which consists of 126 merchants, 80 percent of whom are Italian-Americans. Two of the most important aims of the Association are to preserve the Italian-American ethnic identity of Monte Carmelo and to publicize, as much as possible, the view that the neighborhood is a safe place to be and, of course, to shop.[6] Despite the Association's strong commitment to the community, many of the Italian-American merchants no longer live in the neighborhood.

Another major association is COMCO, the Council of Monte Carmelo Organizations, which is presently directed by a former resident of the community. The job is basically one of political patronage and the person filling the position is a loyal member of the Democratic Party. One often sees the director of COMCO and the Party district captain, who also lives outside of the neighborhood, huddled together in the Democratic Club which is located nextdoor to the COMCO office. "The Council of Monte Carmelo Organizations," according to an active board member (the board member grew up in Monte Carmelo but moved out twenty years ago), "is primarily concerned with maintaining a strong Italian presence in the community." Not only does COMCO function as a social service agency for the elderly and the poor, but it also plays a key role in assisting the "right people" in renting apartments. COMCO was especially active in helping families apply for apartments in a high-rise complex of three buildings located on the eastern border of Monte Carmelo and in a number of recently renovated apartment dwellings.[7]

Besides the Merchants Association and COMCO, there are other community-wide organizations, including the Neighborhood Development Agency which, like COMCO, is a broad-based neighborhood preservation type of association; the Monte Carmelo Italian-American Cultural Association; the Senior Citizens Association; the Italian-American Alliance for Education; the Democratic Club; and a variety of church organizations.

The more prominent organizations, i.e., COMCO, the Merchants Association, the Neighborhood Development Agency, the Senior Citizens Association, and the Democratic Club, comprise an interlocking network of community associations. Two major goals of these organizations are the preservation and revitalization of Monte

Carmelo. One often finds the same individuals serving as officers and board members of these various organizations. What is particularly striking is that a substantial number of these officers and board members live outside the community. In most instances, these are people who are more American oriented than Italian oriented and these are the people who wield the power in Monte Carmelo. An incident that occurred a few years ago clearly demonstrates this. The president of Italy was to visit the community and elaborate arrangements were made to welcome him. It was decided, perhaps for security reasons, to hold the welcoming event at the neighborhood library which also serves as a cultural center. Dignitaries, politicans, community leaders, and others were invited. One of the local leaders[8] wanted to host the event, arguing that his fluency in Italian would make him the ideal choice. He was overruled by the congressman who controls the Democratic Club in Monte Carmelo. The congressman, an American-oriented Italian-American and an "outsider," hosted the welcoming event in English. This was just one of several intra-ethnic confrontations between the locals and the outsiders.

The nexus of the community-based organizations mentioned above, combined with the church, the police, and the racketeer network, is the major structural framework of Monte Carmelo and, as such, plays a crucial role in the maintenance of the Italian-American enclave.


## THE ENCLAVEMENT PROCESS

The issue of the development of an Italian-American enclave in what was formerly a relatively large Italian-American neighborhood requires some discussion of the enclavement process. As mentioned above since the early years of the twentieth century, Monte Carmelo evolved into a predominantly Italian-American neighborhood as large numbers of Italian immigrants and Italian-Americans who had spent some time in other parts of the city settled in the community. For about half a century, the number of Italian-Americans in Monte Carmelo increased substantially as did the spatial boundaries of the community. During the past twenty-five years, however, one is able to discern a dramatic decline in the Italian-American population. Along with this drop in the numbers of Italian-Americans there has been a large influx of Puerto Ricans and Blacks into the neighborhood, in addition to smaller numbers of Albanians and Yugoslavians who have settled in the area in recent times. There are also Irish, Germans, and others of European ancestry, plus small numbers of Koreans, Filipinos, Arabs, Thais, Cubans, and Colombians living in Monte Carmelo.

The most striking change for the Italian-Americans living in Monte Carmelo has been the settlement of Puerto Ricans and Blacks in the neighborhood. As a response, there developed among the Monte Carmelesi a much greater awareness of spatial boundaries. The boundaries of the community are no longer perceived to be what they were in the past. Standing in front of Our Lady of Mount Carmel Church, which serves as the sanctuary of *Italianita*, one can point out the compass boundary markers which encircle an area that today is one-third the size of the traditional Monte Carmelo. The core of the area, the seven blocks with the highest concentration of Italian-American businesses, is also the section that is festooned with red and green decorations and white lights for the late fall and early winter holiday season (Thanksgiving and Christmas) and again in June and July for the feasts of St. Anthony (June 13th) and Our Lady of Mount Carmel (July 16th). The decorative display forms a T with the vertical portion of the T extending for five blocks along Main Street and the horizontal part running a short distance on the south and north sides of Main Street where Main Steet and Market Street interesect. This canopy-like decorative display of colors (which can also be found in the Italian flag) like the church itself with its strong ethnic orientation, continues to express, albeit in an attenuated fashion, the Italian quality of a segment of what was once a fairly large Italian-American neighborhood.

The awareness of spatial boundaries was further accentuated as the frequency and intensity of conflict increased. Although the violence has subsided considerably in recent years, there are still instances of physical violence directed at those who intrude on Italian-American turf. In some cases the victim may be a person who lives within the boundaries of the enclave itself. The victim as a collective symbol of the unwelcomed *stranieri* is reminded of the Italian-American control of the territory. The threat of violence may be sufficient to cower some of the newcomers. Others have been beaten. It is difficult to predict when it will happen, where it will happen, and how it will happen. Most of the people that I have talked to agree that it is much more sporadic and spontaneous than it was in the past. It is not unusual these days to see Blacks and

Puerto Ricans walking along Main Street at all hours of the day or evening. The possibility of violence, however rare, still exists.

The enclavement process as it applies to Monte Carmelo involves not only a greater awareness of spatial boundaries as well as an oppositional posture manifested in real acts of violence and threats of violence, but, in addition, involves cultural and structural aspects. Earlier I had indicated that one could make socio-cultural distinctions within the Italian-American population of Monte Carmelo. Two referential types are used as the basis for distinguishing the range of intra-ethnic variation: the Italian-oriented type and the American-oriented type. There are of course other variants who share, to a greater or lesser degree, traits of the more extreme types. The Italian-oriented type gives the enclave its cultural image, and indeed, one can recognize the Italianness of many of the residents. The American-oriented type, through membership in various community-based organizations and as the personnel in the rackets network, comprise the major structural component of the enclave.[9] These American-oriented Italian-Americans, a number of whom once resided in the community, dominate the economy and the politics of the enclave.

It is this interplay of cultural image and structural matrix, Italian and American variants of the ethnic spectrum, insider and outsider, that helps to maintain Monte Carmelo as the "Little Italy" of the Bronx.

## NOTES

1. The traditional boundaries of the nineteenth-century "village" of Monte Carmelo encompasses an area of five census tracts which have povided me with fairly good population figures covering a period of fifty years. Obviously the Italian-American population was not limited to the five census tracts and contiguous tracts do indicate significant numbers, although considerably less than the figures for the five traditional census tracts.
2. Ethnic violence occurred in the past, especially in the form of "gang wars" between the Italian-Americans and Irish-Americans. In addition, intra-ethnic fights between Italian-Americans from surrounding neighborhoods were not uncommon; and within the community itself, young male immigrants from Italy were frequently bullied by young Italian-American males.
3. There are those who prefer stronger drinks and these are also available.
4. A more extensive discussion of gambling and racketeering appears in Chapter 5.
5. A more extensive discussion of the organizational features of Monte Carmelo will follow in Chapter 5.

6. Many people come from New Jersey, Connecticut, lower Westchester County, and other sections of the Bronx to shop in Monte Carmelo. Some people come just to hang out.

7. In addition to renovating apartment buildings, federally-backed community program efforts have been directed towards the construction of approximately fifty private houses. Those who qualify are required to make a low down payment; and the mortgage rate is well below the going rate. With two or three exceptions, all of the houses have been purchased by Italian-Americans.

8. He has since moved out of the neighborhood but, like many of the others who preceded him, he returns to Monte Carmelo to direct activities at the Senior Citizens Center.

9. The church as an institutional component of the community also plays an important role in Monte Carmelo.

CHAPTER THREE

# The Human Community: People, Places, and Happenings

This chapter describes Monte Carmelo in terms of its people: people in their homes, in other people's homes, in the cafés, in stores, at work, outside the church, and wherever else people gather for a brief exchange of pleasantries, lengthy discussions, or business transactions. People, both individually and collectively, define their social boundaries in terms of interpersonal relationships, and it is in this sense that one can view Monte Carmelo as a human communty affecting the lives of the Monte Carmelesi.

The human community of Monte Carmelo, like a mosaic, is a process of human encounters occurring in time and space. The encounters form the bits and pieces of a general ethnic pattern. It is also something of a kaleidoscope in that the bits and pieces, and the general pattern itself, are in constant flux.

## MR. C.

I first met Mr. C. as I was leaving my apartment to do some shopping. It had stopped snowing a few hours before I had left, and I was concerned about whether the outside steps would be slippery. I was too preoccupied to notice that this elderly man had fallen as he steeped out of the vestibule of the apartment building across the street from where I lived. All I saw was a man looking nonplussed and flailing about with his arms. I went over and helped him up after he had assured me that he did not break any bones. He did ask me, however, to examine the back of his head for any signs of bleeding. Apparently when he fell, the back of his head struck the outside door of the apartment building. I did notice that his left hand was gloved, but not his right hand. I then asked whether he had dropped his right glove; he explained that he had some blood clots removed from his left underarm five months ago and since then he has had difficulty with his left hand.

Mr. C. and I moved slowly through the slush and snow and despite the slow pace he exuded an air of confidence nurtured by sixty-two years of walking the streets of Monte Carmelo. Since he was twenty-two when he literally jumped ship, Mr. C. has been living in the neighborhood.

Mr. C. opened a butcher shop on Market Street and later moved to a new site on Main Street. For sixty-two years he served his many customers, a number of whom came from outside the community. "I worked fourteen to sixteen hours a day, seven days a week. Only later on did I close on Sunday. During the war [World War II] when meat was rationed and butchers were having difficulty getting meat, I always had meat for my customers. Ask anybody who knows me and they will tell you I took care of them. I remember when there were twenty-two butcher shops in Monte Carmelo. There are less now."

Today there are nine fewer butcher shops compared with the halcyon days of the thirties and forties when Monte Carmelo was a bustling Italian-American community. Those were the days when Mr. C. and his wife were raising a family: two sons and a daughter. His sons have since married and left the community. He has been widowed and shares a two-family house on the "Boulevard" with his married daughter. Eastern Boulevard, the "Grand Concourse of Monte Carmelo," was the place to live.

As we walked, people stopped to greet Mr. C., some in English and some in Italian. He proudly expressed his feelings: "You see, the people know me." Mr. C. was also proud of the fact that he played an important role in convincing the officials of Chemical Bank to open a branch in Monte Carmelo. As we passed a pork store, he made a point of telling me that he had trained the owner. "What did he know about making sausages! He came to me to learn."

There were times when Mr. C's face expressed the pathos and the bitterness of life's inexorable passage: his son's leaving the neighborhood; his wife's death; and his recent surgery. "It was the first time that I was in a hospital", he said. "Actually, it was the first time that I was *really* sick." For Mr. C. the illness and the fall were somehow associated with the sale of his butcher shop and his subsequent retirement. Apparently "bad luck" has now creeped into his life. Gazing into the distance, he whispered to himself, "What next?"

There were more greetings, more smiles, as we turned left on Market Street. Storekeepers waved and passersby wished him well. He pointed to a produce stand and told me he was going to the store next to it. I continued walking with him past the stand, stopped momentarily to shake his hand, and left. He turned to go into his friend's butcher shop.

## LOU

It was a cold December afternoon and a group of us were huddled around a heater at J's gas station. Lou, who is in his early seventies, spends a good deal of time at the station. Except for a three-year period, Lou has lived his entire life in Monte Carmelo. We began talking about the past.

His father emigrated from Calabria in 1902, settled in the community, and three years later returned to Italy to marry. He and his Calabrian bride returned to Monte Carmelo soon after the wedding. Lou described his father as a hard worker who often walked from their home in the Bronx to northern Manhattan where he would unload barges for seventy-five cents a day. Like many Italian immigrants of the time, Lou's father had completed three years of schooling in Italy and, consequently, had limited reading and writing skills in Italian and learned to speak and understand very little English over the years. His mother had no formal schooling and could neither read nor write in Italian. She knew practically no English and communicated only in Italian.

Lou managed to complete elementary school. After he reached the age of fourteen it was expected that he would find a job and begin contributing to the support of the family. He became a plumber's helper, earning $14 a week. In many Italian-American households the salaries of sons and daughters were handed over to either the father or the mother for household expenditures.

Lou spoke about the living situation when the was a youngster. When indoors, the family spent most of the time in the kitchen. It was, after all, the warmest room in the house and the kitchen stove was the only source of heat during the cold days. Visitors, who invariably were relatives and friends of the family, often sat around the table drinking espresso or "American" coffee. In the evening Lou's father would light the stove closest to the bedrooms to provide some heat for the sleeping family.

Baths were taken in the kitchen. Each member of the family took a bath on a specific evening while the other members of the family retired to the bedrooms. According to Lou, apartments rented for $40 a month. Today he lives with his common-law wife in a four room apartment which rents for $265 a month.

I asked Lou what it was like growing up in Monte Carmelo. He immediately began telling me how much he enjoyed "hanging-out" and going places with his friends. Apparently the only fly in the ointment were the cops. He described how the cops would harass him and his friends. If the group was socializing on a corner or in front of a store, a policeman would tell them to move on. Lou recalled a particular case of police harassment. Lou and a few other guys jumped into a friend's car for a short drive. One of the young men noticed that they were being followed. Soon the car that was trailing them came alongside and told the driver to pull over. Everyone was ordered out of the car. When Lou got out with his hands up, he was looking into the barrel of a tommy gun. The men with the guns identified themselves as policemen and asked for a driver's license and car registration. One of the cops recognized the name on the license and asked if the driver was related to a particular store owner in Monte Carmelo. Since he was, the police ordered Lou and his friends to "clear out."

Like many of the men of Monte Carmelo, Lou and his freinds enjoyed playing cards. Their card games, however, were frequently interrupted by police raids. The players were forced to lean against the wall and were searched for weapons. Table money was usually "confiscated." Obviously, this proved to be lucrative harassment by the cops which elicited a considerable amount of resentment. The uncertainty and the resentment continues today especially among the more American-oriented Italian-Americans. A number of their clubs are so private and so inconspicuous that few people realize that they exist.

Lou and others of his age set growing up at that time were critical of the police, most of whom were Irish-Americans. The Irish-Americans had been in the general area longer than the Italian-Americans and had settled in neighborhoods to the west and northwest of Monte Carmelo. One middle-aged woman who was raised in the Irish-American community on the "other side of West Boulevard" was warned by her mother "to keep away from those Italians." An Irish-American policeman patrolling an Italian-American neighborhood was not the most propitious way of engendering community trust and respect for the police. The mutual suspicions and hostilities between the two ethnic groups continued to be played out, except that the Irish-American police officer had the full weight of the law behind him. Lou and others like him had to grudgingly concede their powerlessness, though there were those whose influence and money extended beyond the cop on the beat. These were the "big guys" who had wide-ranging gambling interests in the community and used their wealth to insulate themselves from police interference. Gambling is no less popular now, perhaps even more popular, than it was when Lou was a young man. Bookies are as common place as Lotto dealers.

Much of Lou's leisure time as a young man was spent with his male peer group, comprising friends and kinsmen of his age set. There was no equivocation about loyalty. "God forbid if someone did something to one of us." Lou described how a friend who was walking with his girlfriend was offended by a remark made by a young male who was "hanging-out" with his friends in another section of the neighborhood. Recognizing that he was outnumbered, he pretended to ignore the comment and continued walking. When he arrived at his part of the "turf," he told Lou and his other friends about the incident. "Within a short time," Lou recounted, "fifteen to twenty guys piled into a truck and we went looking for the guy who insulted my friend. We knew he was with his friends so we made sure we had enough guys to take care of the situation. We found them and we beat the shit out of them."

Lou's recollections of his youth in Monte Carmelo were generally positive.

We didn't have money but we had fun. People worked hard, but things were so bad during the Depression that we had to go on home relief. At times, things didn't go well between my father and me and he would hit me. I remember when I was about eighteen my father had gotten angry about something and he was about to hit me. I held his arm. He looked surprised and he asked me whether I was going to hit him. I told him I never would and he was never going to hit me again. He never hit my sisters, just me and my brothers. My mother would pinch my arms when I did something wrong. Still, they were good days.

Lou's life consisted of his family, his work, and his friends. Hanging out and going places with his friends were important activities in his life. The home and the street were separate realms: "You never discussed street affairs with your parents." This was probably true of school as well. Although Lou had a limited amount of schooling, what went on in the classroom or the school yard was kept out of the home — it was street business.

Subsequently, Lou married a local girl and had three children. The two girls and the one boy grew up in the neighborhood. All three married and left the community. After his wife died a few years ago, Lou also moved out, but not for very long. He has since returned to Monte Carmelo.

## MICHAEL

During the early months of my field work I spent a considerable amount of time talking to school teachers, paraprofessionals, and school officials. Michael, a one-time neighborhood boy, was the princpal of a local school and I was quite anxious to learn more about him.

Both of his parents were emigrants who settled in Brooklyn in the early 1920s. The youngest of five children, Michael was born in 1935, soon after the family moved to Monte Carmelo. His father worked as a tailor and subsequently opened his own custom tailor shop in Manhattan. Michael described his family as "lower-middle class." He and his two older brothers began working at a young age to help support the family.

Michael went to a local public school for a while and then entered Our Lady of Mount Carmel elementary school. The students at the public school he attended in the early 1940s were Italian, Irish, and Jewish. The school in which he served as chief administrator thirty-five years later consisted of 53 percent Hispanic, mainly Puerto Rican, but including a small percentage of Colombians and Cubans, 30 percent White, and 17 percent Black and others (Arabs and Filipinos). The Italian-Americans comprised 21 percent of the White population and Yugoslavians and Albanians, the remaining 9 percent. He made a point of "how things have changed" since he was a schoolboy in the community.

Michael noted that the SP (Special Progress) classes in the public school that he had attended were made up primarly of Jewish students, and he was one of the few Italian-Americans with a grade average high enough to qualify. Michael's parents, however, took him out of the public school and placed him in the neighborhood Catholic school. Actually, construction of the Catholic school had not been completed and classes were being held in St. Joseph's School for the Deaf. The Our Lady of Mount Carmel school building was officially opened in 1949 and Michael's eighth-grade class was the first to graduate from the new building.

Michael enjoyed sports and he tried to win an athletic scholarship to All Hallows High School but was unsuccessful. This is the way he explained his failure: "It's not that the competition was any better. They were Irish." Attending the local high school was ruled out when his older brother convinced his parents that the school was "poor." So Michael and his other brother attended Cardinal Hayes

High School. After graduating from Hayes he became the youngest
of the three sons attending Fordham University. His interest in
sports continued throughout his college career, during which he
became very active in intermural activities. Like his older brother,
Michael became a teacher and in 1958 secured a position in the
neighborhood Junior high school. He stayed on for eighteen years,
serving as dean and acting assistant principal. When the principal
retired, the assistant principal succeeded him and Michael then
became assistant principal. He stated that the position of principal
should have been his, but indicated that politics dictated otherwise.
The newly-appointed principal had the "appropriate political connections." Apparently, ethnic ties were important political ties as
well. Michael's explanation was that the school district was, admin-
istratively speaking, a "Jewish district." Other ethnics, primarily
Italian-Americans, were given some token recognition. Since the
community had a large concentration of Italian-Americans, a qualified Italian-American should have been given the principal's position. To soften Michael's obvious disappointment, the district superintendent promised him a top administrative position in a school if
he would agree to stay on and work with the new principal. He
remained and a few years later became principal of a newly-
constructed neighborhood school.

Although Michael and his family moved out of the neighborhood
in the early sixties, he continued working in Monte Carmelo until
his death in the fall of 1983. The family purchased a home in a
residential area located in the northeastern section of the Bronx.
Both Michael and his family continued to maintain close ties with
the old neighborhood. His mother often expressed a strong attach-
ment for Monte Carmelo. "She misses the church," Michael explained, "and the Italian-speaking priests to hear confessions." I
mentioned that my parents felt the same way when they moved into
a new neighborhood where the parish priests were Irish and German. Our community at that time had a sizeable Italian-American
population, but the church had no Italian-speaking priests. The
situation that both our families experienced represented a fairly common occurrence among Italian-Americans and other ethnic groups
as well. Families moving out of ethnic enclaves or even larger ethnic
communities frequently moved into new neighborhoods where there
were substantial numbers of their co-ethnics, many of whom were
recent arrivals. The institutional make-up of the community, i.e.,
the school bureaucracy, the church, the local political parties, etc.,

projected a very different ethnic image. Michael's parents and family, like mine, found some solace in the emotional ties and, in some instances, the physical ties that were maintained with the old ethnic neighborhoods.

Michael and his older brother retained their ties with Monte Carmelo over the twenty-three years that elapsed since the family moved from the community: Michael as principal of a public school in the community and as a board member of a number of community-based associations; his brother has a law office, a travel agency, and real estate interests in Monte Carmelo.

Michael, like a number of others that I have met in the community, was born, raised, and educated in Monte Camelo, later moved out but continued to maintain a variety of socio-cultural ties with the old neighborhood. His professional life was primarily spent in the community and his appointment as principal can be partially attributed to community-based political support. For the twenty-two years that Michael lived outside Monte Carmelo, he continued to be an insider. He was privy to a political network, social policy decisions, local job opportunities, and plans for community development. There are others, outsiders who continue to be insiders, who may be less influential than Michael was but, nevertheless, play an important role in the leadership structure of the community. Like Michael, many of them are more American oriented than Italian oriented. This is certainly true of Nick, director of COMCO (Council of Monte Carmelo Organizations), who grew up in the community but left for the "better life" in the suburbs of Long Island. It is also true of Paul who owns a lucrative business on Main Street and heads the Merchants Association.

Michael's commitment to Monte Carmelo was no less strong than his ambition to succeed in his profession or in one of his favorite sports, racquet ball. His interest in the community was lifelong despite the fact that he lived nearly half of his relatively short lifetime outside of it. He was committed to a strong Italian-American presence in Monte Carmelo. He was a board member and fervid supporter of COMCO as well as other community associations. He admitted that one of the major goals of COMCO was (and is) to preserve the "Italian quality" of the neighborhood. To this end, COMCO had been relatively selective in assisting people interested in renting apartments in the high-rise complex located on Eastern Boulevard and in a number of renovated buildings located in various parts of Monte Carmelo. At one point Michael indicated that there were efforts being made to attract Italian-Americans still living in the "famous Little Italy" of lower Manhattan. He also pointed out that there has been some inflow of middle-aged couples who had moved out of the community, raised their children, and returned. He spoke enthusiastically about the future prospects of Monte Carmelo as an ongoing Italian-American community. Despite the fact that he recognized the demographic changes that have occurred during the years that he had taught and served as an administrator in the neighborhood schools, Michael was quite optimistic in his view that the Italian-American population will continue to dominate the community. It is difficult to predict long-term trends, but for the more immediate future anyway, Michael might be right.

In a number of ways Michael's life embodies the American success story as it applies to the immigrant offspring. He worked hard as a youngster, played hard on the ball field, graduated from college, and later became a public school principal. His two older brothers did equally well: the oldest became a school teacher and subsequently earned a law degree at Fordham University; his other brother is an administrator in a large New York-based philanthropic organization and holds the rank of captain in the U.S. Navy Reserve.

In addition to the intellectual skills and psychological attributes that helped Michael in his professional career, there were also the social and political ties which proved to be extremely useful in his appointment to the position of principal in a newly-constructed public school in Monte Carmelo. There was no doubt that he had wanted the top administrative position in the junior high school, where he served as acting vice principal for a number of years, but was passed over for a non-Italian-American. Expressing his disappointment to the district superintendent, Michael implied that the position should have been given to an Italian-American. Over the years, Michael managed to build up a relatively strong power base in Monte Carmelo, primarily through membership in a number of community associations. Furthermore, he had extensive ties with educators and administrators throughout the Bronx and elsewhere as a result of his membership in the Federation of Italian-American Educators (FIAME). It appears to me, however, that his community ties were crucial in his appointment as principal.

To view Monte Carmelo, the traditional neighborhood rather than the enclave, as an Italian-American community is certainly problematical if one were to use demographic data exclusively. The school that Michael headed for eight years had more than twice as many Hispanic students (primarily Puerto Rican) as Italian-American students in 1982. Although these figures are not representative of the proportion of Hispanics, or more specifically the Puerto Rican population, to Italian-Americans they do indicate that the Italian-Americans are no longer the dominant population within the traditional boundaries of Monte Carmelo. The traditional boundaries have shrunk considerably as an ethnic neighborhood developed into an ethnic enclave. Despite the spatial and demographic changes, Italian-Americans still control the political and economic life of Monte Carmelo. And, in many instances, it is the American-oriented Italian-American who is in the more powerful position. More often than not these individuals are Monte Carmelesi who have moved out but maintain ties with the community. Michael was such a person. After spending nearly half his life in the community, he and his family moved. However, he continued working in the community and expanding his network, becoming a member of COMCO, the Merchants Association and other organizations as well. There is no doubt that Michael genuinely loved being around the old neighborhood. His professional talents, being an Italian-American who grew up in Monte Carmelo, and becoming part of its power structure were important considerations in understanding Michael's success story. Michael died as he had lived, playing to win on a racquet ball court.

## VINNY

Vinny and I spent a good deal of time talking about the past. We often met at Carla's Luncheonette for coffee or at Mario's Café for capucchino. Vinny, like many of the young and middle-aged men and women who stop off for coffee, breakfast, or lunch at Carla's place are American-oriented Italian-Americans. It's also a convenient place to play the numbers since one of the collectors often hangs out there.

Vinny was a Depression baby. He was the next to the last child born to Augustino and Anna, both of whom had immigrated from Calabria. Augustino, a carpenter and cabinet maker, had come to the United States as a young man in 1907, then returned to Italy to marry Anna. He and Anna lived in his home town of Nicotera for a few years and then Augustino left for the United States for the second time in 1913. It wasn't until 1920 that Anna and her two daughters were able to join Augustino in New York. After staying with his brother Luigi for a short time, Augustino and his family rented an apartment in East Harlem. Soon after Vinny was born, the family moved to Monte Carmelo.

Since the family was quite large — seven daughters and two sons — it was difficult finding a suitable apartment that was also relatively cheap. Living space was very limited for the family: two bedrooms for the girls; one for the parents; and the boys slept in the living room. In spite of the crowded conditions, members of the family somehow managed to maintain their individual privacy while still sharing in such family-centered activities as the evening meal, the Sunday afternoon *pranzo* (dinner), summer picnics at Orchard Beach or Pelham Bay Park, and the celebrations of holidays and special events.

According to Vinny, the street was the center stage in the daily life drama of a young boy in Monte Carmelo. The early years were characterized by peer play groupings. Vinny described it in this fashion:

Street playing was the single most important focus of my life. My friends and I would play different games depending on the time of year. Summer, of course, was great fun. I can still remember my end-of-school year ritual. We had to clean out our desks and our ink wells. A block or so away from the school I dumped everything down the sewer. It symbolized my break with ten months of confinement and rote-learning. It represented an endless ten weeks, free of the tyranny of a Sister Perpetua or a Sister Theresa.

There were a variety of summer street games, including a team handball game with a pitcher, catcher, and three basemen. The hitter would use the hand as a bat. One of the most popular games was stickball. We often played three games a day: morning, afternoon, and early evening. Two of the better players would choose up sides. One guy would toss the stick to the other who would grip it with one hand. The tosser would place his hand immediately above that of his opponent. This alternation of hand grip would continue until the end of the stick was covered by one of the two team captains. The winner would choose the first teammate who, more often than not, was the third best player in the group. This would continue until the teams were formed. Usually the worst players were the last to be chosen unless, of course, there was a good friend you wanted on your side. Stick-ball games were not only block events but, in some instances, became intra-neighborhood competitive games.

There were other summer street games, including Johnny-on-a-pony, marbles, shooting bottle caps into the square, tag, and Ringoleevio. Sometimes a bunch of us went to the park or the school yard to play basketball, handball, or softball.

For those of us (and there were many) who could not afford a bicycle, we constructed our own recreational vehicle, the box scooter. All one needed was a piece of wood about one-inch thick, six-inches wide, and a couple of feet long; a wooden box; and a discarded skate. Some of us had elaborate scooters with finely carved handles and various designs on the front and sides of the wooden box.

On hot summer days and evenings we opened the fire hydrants. This was illegal so we had to keep our eyes open for the cops. Some things haven't changed very much since I was a boy. Walk around on a hot summer day and you'll notice that many fire hydrants are open. Some are equipped with sprinkler caps which make their use legal; others are not, so there's always someone looking out for the cops.

Autumn was the football season. Touch football was especially popular and few of us escaped the bruises, sprains, and fractures which our bodies sustained when they contacted the concrete streets and sidewalks. Today the kids still throw a football around and some play skate hockey.

The winter snows brought out the architectural skills of some of my friends. They would build snow forts in which to store a large cache of snowballs. The snowballs were used to ward off an "enemy" attack. A battle truce was called whenever a group of girls passed. We would all concentrate our fire on them.

When the professional baseball players began spring training, we would begin limbering up for the stickball and softball season. The warming trend of spring reminded us that summer would soon be here and for me this meant a season of ball playing in the streets, frolicking under open fire hydrants and, on those special days, swimming at Orchard Beach and picnicking in Pelham Bay Park.

Another sport that was fairly popular in the neighborhood was raising and racing pigeons. Usually the older guys were involved though some of us younger ones helped out. My uncle Marco was one of those young men who spent a great amount of time on the roof with his birds. The men joined with others who raced pigeons to form clubs. Club members would drive long distances and release their birds. It wasn't just a matter of winning for the sake of winning. People bet on those pigeons and large sums of money were won and lost. Some birds were prime racers and, according to my uncle, have won thousands of dollars for those who placed bets on them. He himself owned one that had earned more than $60,000 for winning bettors. My uncle no longer lives in Monte Carmelo, but at seventy-five he continues to raise and to race pigeons. He now has another champion.

After a few years in a public school, Vinny was enrolled in a parochial school. For the next dozen years or so he continued in Catholic schools, graduating from Fordham University in the mid-fifties. Vinny no longer lives in Monte Carmelo. Like most of his other siblings, he moved out of the neighborhood after he married. He and his Italian-Ameircan wife rented an apartment in the Pelham Bay section of the Bronx. Within a few years they bought a house in the nearby Country Club section. Vinny returns to the neighborhood to visit his eighty-year-old mother and older sister. He often hangs around to talk to a few of his old friends.

On one occasion I had asked Vinny if he could tell me some things about his mid- and late teens. He went on to talk about a variety of topics.

High school was so much better than elementary school. Maybe it was because the Sister Theresas and Sister Perpetuas were replaced by the Brother Pauls and Brother Gabriels. Basically, I think it's because the nuns were not as well educated as the brothers. Perhaps elementary school teachers were not required to know as much as high school teachers, both in terms of subject matter and teaching methods. It was a totally different world. Yes, discipline was enforced but the techniques were differ-cnt. In my four years of high school, only once do I recall one of my classmates being struck by a teacher, and in that particular instance he was a lay teacher. It was a rare day that three or four kids were not hit by the teacher in elementary school. The whole scenario became a way of life that I carried with me for six frightful years. When I got to high school, the fear had gradually lifted. The fear of being physically abused slowly subsided but a new fear took its place: the fear of not doing well.

Many of my classmates came from various parts of the city and a few commuted from Long Island. The majority were Irish — the Italians comprised a significant minority in the school. I got to be very friendly with a number of Irish kids in my classes, though my best friend, Johnny, was an Italian-American from Monte Carmelo who attended the same high school. My Irish classmates were from middle-class backgrounds and many lived in quiet residential sections of Queens. Their life styles were very different from mine and my relatives.

Ever since I can remember, I had coffee and toast for breakfast. My mother made special coffee and specail toast for us. The night before she would boil a large pot of water and dump the coffee seeds into the water. After the coffee was made she placed a cover on top of the pot and let it sit overnight. She would also slice leftover bread and place it in the oven to toast, then turn off the oven and leave the toast for the next morning. Our breakfast was ready when we got up — scoop up a cup of coffee from the pot and heat it and then open the oven and pull out the most appetizing piece of toast. If you were the last one up, you got the leftover toast, the rejects. Well, that's the sort of breakfast I had for so many years. On Sundays it was different. We usually had cake for breakfast. When I went to visit an Irish classmate from Queens for the weekend, I was fed lamb chops for breakfast. For me, lamb chops were eaten on very special occasions, and most certainly not for breakfast.

One of my most embarrassing experiences occurred when the parents of one of my Irish classmates offered to drive me home. I tried very hard to convince them not to, but they insisted. It was a very uncomfortable ride back to Monte Carmelo for me. I kept thinking about the encounter between my parents and my friend and my friend's parents. My mother spoke only in Italian and understood very little English. My father spoke some English but felt very uncomfortable unless communicating in Italian. Also, both my parents were considerably older than my friend's parents. There was this gnawing feeling of inferiority which became more acute as we approached the neighborhood.

Living in Monte Carmelo, an ethnically distinctive Italian-American neighborhood, with its vibrant street life, cheap, wooden frame houses, and drab tenement-like apartment buildings was considerably different, at least in my mind, from living in the quiet neighborhoods of Queens with the new brick houses and tree-lined streets. My years of friendship with my Irish and German schoolmates had reinforced what had probably developed over a period of time: a rejection of my ethnicity. I wanted to be an American and not Italian or an Italian-American. I spoke Italian — or rather a unique variety of New York Italian — to my parents and English to my siblings, relatives of my generation, and friends. The Italian that I spoke was a Calabrese dialect. I could neither read nor write standard Italian, and my understanding of the dialect was fairly limited. I learned to communicate about relevant topics: how to deal with relatives and merchants, household activities and responsibilities, and earning a living. God, the Madonna, and the saints were also part of our conversational world. Basically, then, the Italian I spoke was a household language and a limited one at that. For me, my parents and their generation were the Italians; symbols of my backwardness. My Irish friend and his parents would bear witness to this fact and the secret that I have kept so closely guarded, entombed so to speak, within the boundaries of Monte Carmelo, would be discovered by my Irish friend and his parents. I did introduce them to my parents. My mother smiled, knowing that there would be virtually no communication between her and them. My father managed to say a few words, feeling awkward and decidedly uncomfortable. The amenities were conducted out on the porch and then my friend and his parents left. He never came to my house again, nor did I invite him to do so. I never spent another weekend with him and his family.

During one of our many meetings, I asked Vinny about his neighborhood friends during his high school years.

Except for Johnny, who attended the same parochial high school as I did, the guys in the neighborhood and the guys in high school constituted two distinct friendship groupings. My neighborhood friends were almost exclusively Italian-Americans, some of whom were high school dropouts. Many of us had part-time jobs in the community and we often hung out together in front of Tony's Candy Store. We would joke around a lot, plan some of our weekend activities, and flirt with the girls who would pass by in groups. Whenever someone's sister or girlfriend was in the group, we were particularly careful about how we talked to the girls. We grew up with most of them and, like many of the guys that I hung out with, the girls were more American than Italian, Occasionally, some of the guys and girls would agree to meet in one of the movie theatres outside of the immediate neighborhood and then pair off for some heavy necking in the balcony. Those of us without dates would spend part of our time watching the movie and the rest of the time watching the kissing. I was especially attracted to Angela. She was about a year older than I and, consequently, I was just a kid to her. But, to me, she was the sexiest seventeen-year-old girl in the neighborhood. And could she kiss! I would watch her and her boyfriend necking in the movie theatre and it would just drive me crazy. Her younger sister Eleanor had a crush on me and Angela tried to fix us up but it was Angela that I wanted, not Eleanor. Angela completed high school and worked as a secretary for a few years before getting married. I haven't seen her for many years. The last I heard she was living in Rockland County.

One of the most popular summer areas for the guys and girls to get together at was Orchard Beach. The girls would tell their parents that they would be going to the beach with their relatives and girlfriends. This was usually an opportunity for the individuals in the group to meet up with their respective girlfriends or boyfriends. These were also opportunities for potential boyfriends and girlfriens to strike up a relationship. Because many people from Monte Carmelo picnicked at Orchard Beach, we tried to avoid those areas.

Sports, girls, and cars were the major topics of conversation. School was a necessary evil and we rarely discussed it. A number of the guys were average students, some had dropped out, and there were those who did very well. Actually, it was the street life and recreational activities in general that kept us together. Besides, many of us had relatives in the group as well.

Back in the fifties some of the guys in the neighborhood were members of the North Avenue Baldies. They were a pertty tough gang and quite a few of them were sent to prison. A number of others died violent deaths. None of my group were members of the Baldies, though some of my friends had relatives who were. Like everyone else in Monte Carmelo we knew the Baldies were a neighborhood gang and we avoided any kind of confrontation with them. The police were obviously interested in their activities but no one was willing to cooperate. Things happened in the neighborhood — a person was murdered or someone was beaten up. Many of us knew the guilty parties and the circumstances of the violent crimes. In fact we often discussed these incidences among ourselves, but we never shared the information with the police or with stangers. Our rule was rather simple: Live your life and mind your own business. When these killings or assaults occurred, we assumed that people were taking care of their business. Things haven't changed very much. You've heard of the recent murders? People are still taking care of their business.

For Vinny, Monte Carmelo continues to be a very special place. He feels more comfortable visiting with his old friends from the neighborhood than he does socializing whith his colleagues in the legal profession. He and his family particularly enjoy attending Midnight Mass at our Lady of Mount Carmel. For Vinny, like others who grew up in the neighborhood and then moved out, the community provides continuity with the past, a symbol of a persistent ethnicity. And there are those who, having left, return to their businesses and their jobs. Vinny belongs to a group who still sustains ties with Monte Carmelo and plays a crucial role in the maintenance of an Italian-American enclave.

## A WARM JULY EVENING OUTSIDE THE ROMANO HOUSE

Mrs. Romano, her twenty-year-old daughter Anna, and a *paesana*, Matilda, were sitting together when I joined them. Mr. Romano had gone to sleep two hours earlier. Since he is up at 4:00 A.M. for an early shift at the Fiorio Biscuit Company, he is often in bed by 9:00 P.M. Mrs. Romano rarely leaves the protective boundaries of her home except for her visits to a clinic for medical treatment.

Half a block away were the sounds of people patronizing the food booths and game booths set up along Main Street, extending from Bishop Perone Square to Market Street. It was the annual Feast of Our Lady of Mount Carmel. Today the merchants and the church officials refer to this type of event as a street festival, but for many of the people it is a *festa*. In June there is the St. Anthony *festa* and in July, Our Lady of Mount Carmel. Past *feste* were much grander according to the Monte Carmelesi. Booths were set up on many more blocks and there were Italian bands playing Italian music. The four blocks of *festa* activity represent just a remnant of what was an extensive social and cultural event. The dwindling space is merely a reflection of the decline in the Italian-American population. Yet twice every year, for two weeks in June and two weeks in July, the booths are there and the lights brighten the dark summer nights. The four blocks of lights and noise are a reminder that the community, however small, continues to be Italian-American territory.

For Mrs. Romano there was little excitement or interest in what was going on half a block from her home. This *festa* cannot compare with those she had participated in while growing up in a moderate-size town about sixty kilometers east of Naples. Feasts lasted three days, with a mass and procession through the town comprising the sacred part of the event. The secular component consisted of game booths, rides, lights, music, and fireworks. Sweets, but not regular food, were sold. Those who wished to eat a meal went to restaurants. People from neighboring towns visited her town during the *festa*. A pained smile came over Mrs. Romano's face as she proudly boasted about how good her town *feste* were. "There were not like the ones you get here. Here they go on for more than a week. Maybe it's because the church makes a lot of money. You know that they have gambling in the church basement. The gambling booths used to be outside the church on the side street. Now they are in the basement."

Her *paesana*, Matilda, nodded in agreement. The church and the priests are often criticized by the Monte Carmelesi. Many rarely go to church, though few acknowledge that total separation from the church would be an acceptable way of life. Men and women, young and old, recognize that the church plays an important role in the cycle of life. The intimate relationship between Catholic rituals and the significant life events is one of the enduring characteristics of the Italian-American population. Baptism, first holy communion, confirmation, marriage, and the funeral mass are the rituals that tie the individual to the church. The *festa* is more of a communal expression of identity and, as such, links the church to the people.

Mrs. Romano, her daughter, Anna, and her *paesana*, Matilda, clearly recognize the significance of the life cycle rituals, despite their criticisms of particular priests or church policy. And Matilda, like many other parents in the neighborhood, sends her children to parochial school.

We talked on into the late evening. Mrs. Romano excused herself, as she had grown tired and wanted to go to sleep. Matilda, Anna, and I stayed on to converse about women and their roles in society.

Young Anna certainly typifies the more Italian-oriented women in the community. After completing high school, she received some training in computers in order to develop marketable skills in a relatively short period of time. This is reminiscent of earlier days when a large number of Italian-American women graduated from high school with vocational diplomas and then went on for some training in a secretarial school. The purpose was to learn a skill quickly, secure a job for a few years, and then get married. This is precisely what Anna would like to see happen, but there are problems.

It's very difficult for me to meet a guy. How can I? I hardly go out. If I do, my parents must know where I go, who I go with, and when I will be home. If I'm going to be with guys at a disco place, I try to convince my parents that I'm *really* going out with my cousins and friends. All of us have curfews. My mother always waits up for me. My father is usually asleep, but he knows my mother will be waiting. This happens to my friends and cousins also. If I get in too late, then I'm not allowed out for a while. Some of my friends have been hit for coming home after curfew. One of my friends who goes to college has told me how difficult it has been for her to get along with her parents. She's told me that she would like to leave and get her own place. I think she's crazy. Why would you leave your family? Really! How can you leave your family? I couldn't, no matter how bad things get. Maybe they're old fashioned. Maybe they don't understand that life is different here. Maybe they *can't* understand. Anyway, my mother needs me; my father does too.

Despite the fact that her mother is very ill and does need her daughter to help around the house, Anna still looks forward to marriage and a family. She enjoys caring for Matilda's three-year-old son, and when her married sister visits, Anna often plays with her young niece and nephew. She has another sister, the eldest, who lived upstairs but moved to Italy three years ago.

Matilda, a woman in her thirties, also reflects the more Italian-oriented type woman. Her husband works in a bakery during the late evening and early morning hours, and she works in a hospital kitchen during the day. A considerable number of Italian-oriented women in the community work, and quite often the kind of work they do is associated with women's traditional activities — some work in the kitchens of institutions, others in local sweat shops as seamstresses.

We talked about how some women have rejected the more traditional expectations of their parents. Matilda described what happened to one of her friends.

She grew up like many of the girls I knew. Her parents were strict with her. She finished high school, got a job, and stayed with her parents. You only leave your parents' home when you marry or you die. Otherwise you stay, no matter what. My friend met this fellow and they began living together. Well, her parents just completely rejected her. This was a terrible disgrace to them and to the family. People talked; the neighbors and relatives gossiped. What was worse, she got pregnant. When she gave birth to twins her parents wanted a reconciliation. My friend refused their offer. Now she's alone with her two children and had to go on welfare.

Matilda visits her friend and gives her some pointers on child care. In Italy, however, this would not be the case.

I wouldn't be friendly with her if this happened in my town. My relatives and the neighbors would talk about me. They would think that I would act as she did. They would call her a *puttana* (slut). Here it is different. I'm sure some people would still call her a *puttana*, but there isn't that kind of pressure to avoid associating with her. I have no relatives here — just a few *paesani*. Anyway, I feel sorry for the woman, and the babies are so cute. I told her she should accept her parents' offer to help. She should forgive and forget. After all, her parents are willing to.

Later in the evening Matilda's young teenage daughter joined us. She had just returned from spending some time at the feast and was pressuring her mother to allow her to go back to listen to the music. Matilda refused. The daughter persisted in her pleas but Matilda was firm. She had permitted her to stay out later than usual because it was a special occasion. Finally, the young girl realized that her mother would not budge, so she sat on one of the steps listening to the distant music and waited for her mother to go upstairs.

Matilda and her husband, Sal, find it difficult to adjust to American society, even in a community where Italian traditions are fairly commonplace. The children communicate with their parents and their parents' *paesani* in Italian but speak to one another and to their friends in English. At one point, Sal stated that he had "lost" his daughter to the American way and that this was about to happen to his son who is a few years younger than his daughter. He was debating whether to send him to Italy to complete his education. I'm certain Sal has often thought about returning to Italy with his family. Matilda, also, has expressed her dissatisfaction and disappointment with her life in Monte Carmelo: "What have I got here? A few small rooms and that's it. At least there I have a house and some land. I can grow things. It's a palace compared to this."

Sal, perhaps more so than Matilda, has expressed his intentions to change things for himself and his family. A neighbor has described Sal as a "talker," someone who intends to do something but doesn't. He did not send his son to Italy. He did not move his family to Italy, though Sal managed a six-week visit recently. He did not purchase a home in the Eastchester Avenue vicinity of the Bronx despite numerous indications that he was determined to do so.

Perhaps Sal is a "talker," but he is a hard worker. I have been told that his primary interest is in *danaro* (money). He often works seven days a week, rarely taking time off from his job in a bakery. There's no doubt that Sal and Matilda are putting money away. A combined income of over $30,000, a low rent, and modest living expenditures in general, make for a hefty savings. Ultimately Sal and his family will make a move. It's very likely that it will be to a two-family house in the north-eastern part of Bronx with enough land for a small garden.

## THERESA

I first met Theresa in a candy store on Main Street. Since I knew the owner, I stopped by from time to time. I soon discovered that Theresa was the proprietor's godchild and, therefore, he had a special interest in her welfare.

At fifteen, Theresa is the youngest of seven children who range in age from fifteen to thirty-two. Her seventeen-year-old brother will be the first of her siblings to complete high school — five of her brothers and sisters dropped out after the tenth grade. Her parents had very little formal education. She hopes to get a high school diploma and then enroll in college courses in order to become a paraprofessional. Theresa has attended the local elementary and junior high schools but, like so many Monte Carmelesi of her age, she will not go to the neighborhood high school because the ethnic composition is primarily Black and Puerto Rican.

The Italian-Americans who attend public high school travel out of the neighborhood. They virtually bus themselves out. It is rather ironic that the Black and Puerto Rican students, who were being bussed in seventeen or eighteen years ago, became the antagonists in a brutal confrontation which spread violence and hatred throughout Monte Carmelo. Now the Italian-Americans have turned their backs on the neighhorhood high school and are going elsewhere. Theresa and her friends will be going to Columbus High School.

Theresa's commitment to education, as reflected in her actions, is minimal. She often cuts classes and rarely does any school work. She enjoys hanging-out with her friends and spends a considerable amount of time interacting with boys. Theresa, and others like her, comprise bi-gender peer groups who have favorite hang-out places. These young men and women are primarily American-oriented Italian-Americans.

Unlike Anna who rarely, if ever, questions her parents' wishes and would consider disobedience a brazen act of disrespect, Theresa is blatantly defiant. One day her father came into the candy store and demanded that she go home. She refused. He then threatened her. Again, she refused. He looked at me and then at her. "Wait until I get you upstairs," he said. As he left, she said under her breath, "Fuck you!" She admitted that she dislikes her father very much and she acknowledged that he often beats her.

It reminded me of other such situations both past and present. Somehow a mother striking her child seems to be more acceptable. But a father hitting a daughter, especially an older daughter, generates bitterness and even hatred. Theresa's eyes were filled with hate. She no longer flinched at the prospect of being beaten. Even in the candy store she had expected that her father would strike her. He didn't, but she knew it would happen later and she was determined to stay out as long as possible. She realized that it would make very little difference whether she returned home late since she would be punished for her disobedience anyway.

Theresa is not the only young woman who has been physically punished for disobedience. Disobedience is viewed as an intolerable act of disrespect, and being disrespectful is interpreted as a grave character flaw. Girls, and women in general, are expected to be obedient and submissive. In addition, they appear to be much more intimidated by threats of physical punishment. A number of them are genuinely afraid of their fathers. They are frightened by the prospect of being beaten. There are those, of course, who have a warm, loving, and trusting relationship with their fathers and rarely, if ever, are physically punished. For Theresa and a number of others this is not the case.

Theresa's situation, although not representative of what happens when a young woman disobeys her father, does invite a certain amount of speculation about the circumstances that might contribute to such a conflict-ridden father-daughter relationship. There are, obviously, personality factors that would have to be considered; but beyond that, the socio-cultural context provides the form for the expression of interpersonal relationships. Obviously, Theresa and her father have very different perceptions of the world. He immigrated from Italy after spending his formative years and his young adult life in a small town in southern Apulia. Theresa grew up in Monte Carmelo. The father expects his daughter to spend time doing household chores after school. Theresa prefers socializing with her friends, frequently cutting classes to do so. Her father demands that his daughter's behavior conforms to his standards of how a young woman should act. Yet, Theresa smokes, often hangs out with a group of young men, and occasionally demonstrates a certain fondness for public displays. During the Feast of Saint

Anthony, while being carried piggyback by a young man, Theresa was trying to get the attention of her friends. It was obvious that many other people in the area were equally aware of what was happening.

Theresa's behavior contradicts most, if not all, of her father's expectations. He was reared anticipating very specific gender-related behavior by his wife, his sons, and his daughters. Yet life in Monte Carmelo provides enough variation to accommodate different styles of living. In becoming more American oriented, Theresa has antagonized her father, and by challenging his authority, has cast a shadow on him and his family by her public displays of disrespect. His image tainted, he strikes out at her physically and verbally.

Other young women have shared similar experiences. A twenty-year-old college senior "was thrown out" of her home by her father. Her mother was also ejected. It was expected that mother and daughter would stay with relatives for a few days and then return home. The mother did return but the daughter refused. Although the father pleaded with her, she was determined to live on her own. For him, a daughter living on her own would surely be labeled a *putanna*. His pleas and promises having failed, he became so enraged that he accosted her on the street and began to throttle her. His fury subsided as quickly as it began. Some time after this incident there was a rapprochement between father and daughter. She has since returned home but, according to her, "on my terms."

Theresa and the college senior perceive the world differently than do their parents. To a certain degree this is probably true of Anna as well. Anna, however, has maintained closer ties with Italian-oriented individuals and their traditions. Moreover, her goals are quite compatible with those that her parents have for her. Perhaps her greater conformity could be attributed to the fact that her mother is very ill and needs her. I have heard from others that she often bemoans the fact that "life and love" are passing her by. Recently she stated that she wants to get involved with a man "even if I get hurt."

Theresa and Anna evidence some of the variations in the life styles of the young women in Monte Carmelo. Neither one is meant to be a representative type. Each is merely expressive of a variant in a mosaic of life styles. Although the mosaic, like a kaleidoscope, is in constant flux, there are some persistent patterns which, when formulated as "ideal types," provide us with parameters for viewing the shades of differences. With this in mind, one can characterize Theresa as a more American-oriented Italian-American (or less Italian oriented) and Anna as a more Italian-oriented Italian-American (or less American oriented).


## FRANK

A man in his mid-sixties, Frank is facing what he calls the "alienation of the aged." Here is a man who is not only reflecting on his life, but on life in general. He is philosopher, social critic, and cynic who has lived most of his life in Monte Carmelo.

My parents emigrated from Agerola in the Naples area and were married here. The stories about America were always prevalent at all times, being that they needed laborers, and they tried to encourage an immigration from the lower economy areas into America for exploitative reasons. They needed slobs. In a chiselocracy there are only two classes of people: chiselers and suckers and the suckers have to come from the low economy areas.

Some of my uncles were here already and, naturally, many of the *paesani*. Many of the people from the area had preceded them and the word got around. This is the way I think most of them came over. They came to those who had come before them and they came into their own little communities. They expected to find gold, figuratively speaking, out in the streets and you'll find this is still going on. You have Italian laborers that go to Switzerland, Italian laborers that even go so far as to Russia. And of course, they come from other areas too. You have low economy areas or low speed economy areas and high speed economy areas such as our highly industrialized areas. And that's the name of the game. Chiselers and suckers.

My father went to live with relatives in the Village. My parents were married and then the family moved to 116th Street and Pleasant Avenue, and finally they came up to the Bronx which was the suburban area of the days. My father came here because he had a business opportunity.

In those days Monte Carmelo was in the true sense a community. If you lived in an apartment house, you were free to go into almost any apartment as a child and be accorded the same type of treatment that they would give to their own children. I don't remember doors being as locked as they are now, naturally, but when holidays like Easter and Christmas came around we as kids went from one aunt to an uncle. We made the rounds. Today there is much more alienation. In fact, in my day when I was a youngster, if you missed mass on a Sunday, almost the whole neighborhood knew it because the church was the center of all activity at that particular time. Yes, there was a community spirit. We knew everybody.

As a kid, I was an altarboy. Not that I want to brag, but we were given Latin to learn in two weeks and I learned it overnight and as a consequence, became the pride and joy of Father Camini and, of course, that built up some aspirations on my part to be a priest. One of the mistakes I made was to take religion too seriously because I discovered now, in looking back, that this is a nation that teaches and preaches Christianity and punishes those who practice it. I recall many times going out with Father Camini looking for needy cases and helping them out to the extent possible, which is something that is surely lacking now. But I don't want to put myself in a position now to be a critic of the church. They don't need any critics now because they're sealing their own doom.

Frank attended the local public high schools and took some courses at New York University. He had some rather critical comments to make about education.

As far as schools were concerned, they were glorified jails. Now they're glorified snake pits. Now, when I went to public school, the principal glorified the activities that were waiting for us as Italians, as though we had no possibility of being anything other than carpenters, street diggers, working in factories or what have you. They never played up doctors or lawyers or encouraged aspirations to be one of those. No, we were always projected to be nothing more than laborers. Now, as far as learning everything that I learned, I had to unlearn and, unfortunately, I haven't been able to unlearn all the indoctrinations in school and it's very difficult for anybody to unlearn because there is so much reenforcement of all this bad knowledge, and I use "bad" with quotation marks.

Frank began working at nearly the same age that he started school.

I think I must have been about eight years old when I had my first job and it was merely a matter of coming from upstairs to downstairs. We had a factory underneath where we lived, where in fact I'm living now. So, my father was a robe and sportswear contractor and as long as I was tall enough to reach the treadle on the sewing machine I was put to work. In order to engage in any play activities after school, I always had to invent reasons, otherwise my father would have me at the machine all day long. In those days the work week was seventy-eight hours, Saturdays and Sundays, it made no difference. That was prior, of course, to the Depression. When the Depression came, there was no work at any time.

Frank recalled the Depression days.

Things were bad. Hold-ups almost every other day. Would-be racketeers were throwing their weight around. Gunfights. So many harsh experiences. When the policemen came around, they didn't come over and put their arms around you affectionately, call you by your name or whatever. It was always the bat; it was always the boot. It was one way or another.

There were those storekeepers who were sympathetic to the problems of the neighbors and you had those who exploited all the way and didn't care how they did it. You had those who sold $2 items for $50 and made you pay 25 cents a week for the rest of your life. And you had those who would give you baskets of fruit if you weren't working or if you were sick and you were financially stressed at the time and told you to forget about it. But, as I said, the hard experiences seem to stand out.

I voted for Roosevelt. I fell in love with his slogan, "Rendezvous with Destiny," and being philosophical and highly idealistic at the time, naturally it seemed to capture my imagination and I went whole hog. When I learned that he paid farmers not to grow and pigs were killed at birth while one-third of the nation was ill-housed, ill-dressed, ill-fed, and the whole nation itself was in dire distress, and he permitted those policies to take place, my disillusionment could only find an outlet in trying to vote him out. So, I voted for Willkie. I believe not because I was for Willkie, but more so because I was against Roosevelt at that time. Voting for Roosevelt and against him were the two times that I voted in my life.

During the Depression some of the kids left the neighborhood to go down South to get out of the winter of New York. They were picked up in some of the southern states and put in chain gangs where they were actually chained, linked one to another and confined there to do brutal manual labor. Now, fortunately for me, I happened to go to California in 1935. I went by motorcycle. I was stopped for a red light one day and I heard someone call my name. I turned and it was two of the fellows from the neighborhood who had gone there. Well, we made an appointment for that evening. I left a few dollars with them to have something to eat and when I went to meet them that night, I couldn't find them. It wasn't until six months later when I returned home and saw them that I mentioned that evening. He said, "Well, we got picked up right after we came out of the restaurant, and they sent us to jail. Then they brought us to the boundary line, they gave us a boot in the fanny and sent us scurrying and said, 'If we find you back in California again, there will be hell to pay.'" Now, I don't blame the Californians for trying to protect themselves, but I do blame the educational system that made me believe that this was one country. Incidentally, it's not one country. We have so many countries here as we have police departments. Every police department is a nation unto itself.

Frank described his feelings about his sense of ethnic identity and his neighborhood.

If you say a person born in Italy is Italian, I'm a North American because I was born on the North American continent. Today it's continentalism, not provincial communities and things like that. A community could be a family. I'm not degrading or minimizing the impact that it could have on a person's growth, the joy that one could find in life because we're gregarious. We're social animals and we need the companionships and relationships with other human beings. Now, when we say Italian, is it my name that makes me Italian or am I a North American with an Italian name? If I take a ruler and measure a sheet of paper and find that it's 8½-by-11, well, I have some standard to go by. I have some measuring implement by which I could evaluate when we say Italian, what do we mean by Italian?

Having been in this neighborhood for many years, I feel it is one of the best and I have to qualify that by saying, for me. Naturally, I feel at home here having been here almost fifty-eight years. I know I have a strong sense of security being in this community than I imagine I would have elsewhere. Of course, I can't speak for any other places than those that I've been to, and since I haven't been to those places recently, I'm not even qualified to mention any other place. But, as far as the neighborhood is concerned, I feel it has anything I could need as a human being. At least, it offers it. It gives me my privacy, it gives me my companionship. But, I imagine, this could be said of any close-knit neighborhood.

You could call this neighborhood the Little Italy of the Bronx. The fact that you have a heavy concentration of Italians would make it Little Italy. Pretty soon you may be able to call it also the Little Puerto Rico of the Bronx.

My own block is important to me. We could spend a whole lifetime on one block and not feel that we missed out on anything. I've been to various places in this world. I've seen different trees and yet they're all the same. Not only that, but five seconds after you leave any specific site, the new sites impinge on your consciousness and force all the other ones into the background. Just being with a few people in your own little neighborhood is more than enough to satisfy a life, the way it did with our grandparents and their grandparents.

I'm a prisoner of the community and I say it joyously. Occasionally, I venture outside the neighborhood, but not too far. I'm having some battles with old age and one of the battles of old age is to seek security. The blanket over the head seems to be the best possibility for feeling secure so you try to stay as close to homegrounds as possible. Now I am afraid to venture outside my own community. There are various reasons. There are the anxieties and the phobias that you have to deal with but as much as I hate the terror of old age and the alienation and the isolation that goes with it, there's no way I could turn back.

# FRANCES

Frances is a young woman in her mid-twenties. Her parents emigrated from Siano, a town near Salerno, in the mid-fifties. They lived in East Harlem for about two years and then moved to Monte Carmelo where Frances was born in July of 1957. She attended Catholic schools: elementary school, high school, and college. Frances describes aspects of her educational experiences and discusses her impressions of the neighborhood.

When I went to high school, I didn't really have that much of a hard time. I was fairly prepared. English is the only thing, I'm not talking about English speaking. Well, I guess it's a problem with all schools now. They didn't emphasize the grammar as much but, other than that, the discipline wasn't that bad.

I realized when I went to Fordham that I was able to read Shakespeare and all the great authors, but I couldn't express my thoughts in proper English. The high school I went to should have put more emphasis on grammar. It was a pretty good high school. What could you expect from an all-girl Catholic high school. We had our times. There are a lot of girls from the neighborhood who go there because it's right in the neighborhood.

When I was in high school, most of the girls in my classes were Italians. By the time I graduated, things were changing. I see the changes in that we have a lot of new people coming in, like Yugoslavian and Albanian people. We have Puerto Rican stores; we have these Yugoslavian and Albanian stores. But, they're just there to cater to their own people because Monte Carmelo isn't just predominantly Italian anymore. We've been infiltrated.

My mother's been in this neighborhood for twenty years. She speaks English, but very badly. For somebody who lived in a country for so many years, you kinda figure she would be fluent, but since Market Street and Main Street is predominantly Italian my mother was never forced to learn English because whatever store she went into people understood her. Even the Jews like Cohen Brothers. They all speak Italian. My mother never left Italy. She came from one Italy to another, so I have to speak Italian to her. She understands English. It's strange because my brothers speak English to her, but I speak Italian.

I have friends that don't speak Italian and friends that do. Usually the girls I grew up with or the guys will say Italian things to each other. Or, if we don't want somebody to understand, we'd speak Italian.

I really like this neighborhood. It's home. Sometimes I get annoyed because everybody knows your business. You do one thing and the whole neighborhood will know about it. You can't hide anything, but it's nice. It's nice when you walk down the street and you know everybody and everybody knows you. I can go into any store and they remember when I was a little girl, so I have a nice feeling for this neighborhood. It's home. Sometimes I see my friends who live in these big beautiful houses, but they live out in the country. There's nobody there. If you want to take a walk, you walk with a squirrel. Here, whenever you're lonely or you're down, just walk downstairs and you're always bound to meet someone. All my friends are here. I have a lot of family. You know, it's the people who make up the neighborhood.

This is the Little Italy of the Bronx. You can buy any kind of Italian food here. Besides that, if you want Italian shoes, you have Italian shoes. We have pork stores. We have Italian people. The majority of people here speak Italian. There are a lot of traditional characteristics here. I was brought up very strictly and, if you don't call that Italian, I don't know what is. When my parents left Italy they brought their traditions and their way of thinking here. Since you're in a new country, you're afraid to change because you don't know anything else. So you hold on to what you know. My parents never changed. They always held on to their way of thinking and that's the way they brought me up.

When I was younger, I used to spend my free time walking up and down Main Street. I still do, but not as often. We used to walk up and down in front of the cafés and look here and look there. You can spend your free time in the neighborhood like a lot of the people who just hang out. Since I got my license, I'm able to go outside the neighborhood and spend my time. When I can't, I hang out.

Getting an education was important to me. My purpose in going to school wasn't because I wanted to find a better job. You know, I'm a girl and I don't need to support myself for the rest of my life. That's usually up to the guy, so in a sense it wasn't necessary for me to go to school to find a good job. I just feel that a person should try to expand himself as much as possible and going to school and getting a college degree is the best way of doing it.

Some of my girlfriends right out of high school went out to work and they're bringing home the $200 a week. But, I always tell them: "Some day you're going to be my secretaries." They're always going to be secretaries for the rest of their lives. How could you progress? Alright, I may start off as a secretary, too; but I have a much better chance of progressing than they do. I think that the majority of people today want their kids to go to school because they don't want their kids to be ignorant and they don't want their kids to be looked down upon. That's the way my mother and father are.

I know a person who came from Italy and doesn't have much of an education and her husband has a college degree. You know, the worst thing is when a husband looks down on you because you're not intelligent or can't understand some things. I would never want it thrown up in my face: you don't understand; you never heard of this. Yeah, I heard of it and I understand. That's all that counts with me, an education. I hate being made to feel inferior.

As Frances describes it, she has recently "found" a boyfriend, an event which shook her loose from a melancholy that had enveloped her life for the past year. This obviously means marriage and a move out of the community.

One needs a change. I know stability is something positive, but I just want to get away. The neighborhood is not going to get any better. If anything, it's deteriorating. It's sad that it is and maybe people like me are the ones that are going to help it go down the drain. The only way I'd move out of the neighborhood is if I get married. I would say I can't move out other than that. And with marriage it's like starting a new life. So I think you have to start afresh. If you live in the neighborhood after marriage, it looks like nothing has changed in your life. The only reason I would move away is just for the change; but, I would always come back.

Frances spoke about the church, the priests, and the feasts.

I don't go to church regularly but I am a religious person. I just don't like Mount Carmel Church. The purpose of being a Catholic isn't in the giving of donations. Every time I go there I get so mad. You're not supposed to go to church to get mad. When you go there Christmas Eve you want to hear about the birth of Christ, not that there's going to be two collections. You know it's sad. A lot of times I read the Bible and stuff, but I just get very mad going to Mt. Carmel because I think they completely, *completely* lost contact with Christianity. Everybody is in an economical bind, but you don't come out and say, "Alright, the bigger donation you give, the more God will bless you." It is as if you're buying grace. I don't know if I'm wrong. I may go to hell for this but I don't think so. When I spoke to a priest at Fordham I told him how I felt and that I think I'm a moral and religious person because I don't do anything wrong. I don't go fooling around with every Tom, Dick, and Harry. I have my values. I just don't seem to care for the neighborhood church. He told me I could always go to Fordham. And I have gone. It's excellent. Those priests are outrageous. I went to confession, face-to-face, something which I thought I would never do. Going to Mount Carmel for confession petrified me. We all sin. We all have to be forgiven. Don't make it sound as if you've committed a crime. "Why did you sin?" How am I supposed to know why I sinned or why I did this. I just did it. It's part of human nature. But going face-to-face I tell them what I did and the priests at Fordham tell you that it's natural to be human. Not sinful. If you go to Father P. at Mount Carmel he would say: "Why did you do it? You should be ashamed of yourself."

Frances's criticisms extended to the community feasts as well.

They're just money-makers for Mount Carmel. There's a thing in the Bible when Jesus went into the temple and saw them all set up selling things. What did he do? He destroyed them. He threw them all out. He doesn't advocate that. If you have feasts and stuff, it shouldn't be as money oriented as it is. In Italy, they have beautiful feasts. Completely different than this. Its not, "We have to get money for the church; we need money for this." It's just a way of gathering people together. It still has the religious purpose behind it. Processions have been going on for centuries. The feasts we have here go on for thirteen days. What is that? Come on, how many times can you walk up and down? It used to be so much bigger and so much better. It used to offer more.

## THE KILLINGS

Monte Carmelo is purported to be one of the safest communities in the Bronx, indeed, in the entire nation. Merchants are quick to tout its secure boundaries and to remind potential customers that they can shop in a worry-free environment. Newspapers have picked up on this theme in numerous articles that have appeared over the past few years.[1]

Even before I became aware of a number of homicides, my suspicions were raised that perhaps Monte Carmelo is not nearly as crime free as all the publicity would lead one to believe. I had just visited a friend on the block next to mine. We were talking outside her house when a woman living next door opened her window and told us that her newly purchased television had been stolen. The television was bought in a local appliance store and had been delivered that very day. She had only left her apartment for an hour or so after it arrived. When she returned, it was gone. With tears in her eyes she bitterly denounced the thieves and swore that she would move out of this "lousy neighborhood." My friend and I speculated that it was probably an "inside job," a theft by someone from the neighborhood or perhaps from the same building. I doubt whether the robbery was ever reported to the police.

Over the past three years, a number of violent crimes have occurred in Monte Carmelo. A young Puerto Rican male was killed on Main Street by a man identified as an Albanian by some of the people. The victim was stabbed and shot. Why? Perhaps it was the result of an argument that ended in bloodshed or an act of violence fostered by an atmosphere of inter-ethnic antagonisms. Albanians and Yugoslavians identify primarily with Italians (and Italian-Americans), perceiving themselves as collectively different from Puerto Ricans and Blacks. The circumstances that triggered the act of violence were exacerbated by the ethnic identity of the victim. One middle-aged woman who spoke to me about the murder did not appear too disturbed by it. It was merely an act of violence involving two men who were caught up in a situation which ultimately resulted in the death of one of the two. It was a private matter rather than a public issue, despite the fact that communal attitudes and practices relating to various ethnic populations do indeed affect how specific individuals from different ethnic backgrounds respond to one another in specific situations. If the victim also had been Albanian, the crime itself would still be viewed as a private act, maybe a vendetta for some past affront.

This woman, and others that I spoke to, accept violence as a component of life in Monte Carmelo, providing it is not a random phenomenon. A mugger or would-be rapist who lurks about waiting for a victim to assault is the sort of criminal that becomes a public issue and public threat. Muggers and potential rapists who have been caught by people in the community have been severely beaten, some so brutally that they have been hospitalized with serious injuries. One man in his early twenties reported on a mugging incident.

This girl was coming home from work. A guy ran up to her and ripped off her gold necklace. When she started screaming, he ran towards the park. The poort bastard didn't know the neighborhood too well. He ran right into a bunch of us. We beat the shit out of him. I don't know if anyone called the cops. Actually, he needed an ambulance. We just left him.

One of the most talked about crimes in recent years involved a double murder, an attempted murder which left the victim totally paralyzed, and the alleged suicide of the murderer while in prison.

Like the mugger and would-be rapist who often choose their victims somewhat randomly and, consequently, become a public threat, the case noted above was more of a public issue and, therefore, raised questions which in turn invited a considerable amount of speculation. The "suicide" of the murderer conveniently ended any long-term legal repercussions.

From time to time some unusual happenings occur in Monte Carmelo and more often than not they seem to end as inexplicably as they begin. Not long ago a number of stores and social clubs were robbed. People were puzzled about the robberies since it generally had been recognized that a pattern of such crimes within the neighborhood was a rarity. Some time ago, for example, apartments in a building across from me were being burglarized. Some of the neighbors formed an ad hoc anti-burglary patrol. A few of the men set a trap for the burglar and caught him. After a punitory thrashing, the burglar was led unceremoniously into the street and placed over a sewer. He was then told in no uncertain terms that he had better stay clear of the neighborhood. The warning was couched in these terms: "If we catch you, the beating will be twice as bad and we'll let you rot in the sewer." Although the police were not involved in the case, there have been no burglaries in the building since then.

The recent robberies of some stores and social clubs proved to be more perplexing and unusually complicated. Businesses were now being targeted and gambling interests, more specifically, social clubs with slot machines and high-stake card games, were being threatened. Soon after the spate of robberies, the double murders and the wounding mentioned above occurred. All three victims had been implicated in the robberies according to the views of those I spoke to in the neighborhood. The killer was well known to a number of people — a man in his early twenties, he was considered to be *pazzo* (crazy). After the killings, he continued to move about Monte Carmelo freely, hanging out with his friends and carrying out his daily routine with his usual aplomb. If the police were unaware that he was the killer, many of the Monte Carmelesi were not. It appeared as if he was going to get away with it until one day he walked into a local police station and turned himself in. Soon after, it was reported that he had hanged himself. Few believe that he had actually committed suicide, despite the general impression that he was an unstable person. Such a person was an ideal candidate for a "hit man" job: he had been involved in petty criminal activities; he was described as mentally "slow"; and he was emotionally disturbed. There were those who speculated that he was hired to execute the thieves. Interestingly, not all three were summarily killed. One was critically wounded and lies paralyzed in a hospital bed. The dead somehow are quickly forgotten, but the paralyzed victim is a graphic reminder of the consequences of challenging, powerful interest groups. Or perhaps the victim was shot and left for dead.

There are those who suggest that the killer was one of the gang of thieves and he wanted to eliminate his accomplices to avoid being implicated by them. He feared local retribution more than the legal consequences of his crimes. It was the certainty of reprisal that sent him scurrying to the local precinct. He was subsequently sent to Rikers Island where he was found hanging in his cell. Death has forever silenced the truth. No one will know for certain the circumstances that led to the shootings and the suicide or murder. People will continue to speculate and the merchants and café owners will continue with business as usual, knowing that justice has been served.

There have been other killings over the past three years. One evening after I had parked my car and began walking towards my apartment, a friend called to me and asked whether I had heard about what happened in the early hours of the morning in front of the Café Milano. The body of a man in his twenties was found slumped in a seat with his head resting on the edge of a table. His throat had been slashed. There were no witnesses, or at least no one claimed to see anything. Whenever I pass the Café Milano in the late evening or early morning hours, there are always people playing cards, or drinking an aperitif, or simply hanging-out. It is unlikely that no one had seen what happened. What appears to be more credible is that those in and around the Café pretended not to have seen anything.

Once again people speculated about the motives behind the crime. The victim was supposedly involved in illegal activities or at least some of his family were. His murder was attributed to "crossing the wrong people," though no one seemed to know what he had done. Those people I spoke to viewed the crime as a private vendetta involving specific individuals who were "taking care of their business." If there were witnesses they simply removed themselves from this private scene, i.e., the murder scene, by either looking away or walking away. It was no concern of theirs. To make such a private act a public issue would be a dangerous thing. Fear also plays an important role in silencing people. One can just as quickly become a victim by intruding into the private affairs of others. People from the community have been murdered outside of Monte Carmelo. Two Monte Carmelesi were found shot to death in the Throgs Neck section of the Bronx. One of the victims, a woman in her thirties, worked for a community organization in Monte Carmelo. According to her friends, she had left a Christmas party with her common-law husband to meet someone. Those I discussed the murders with stated that the man was "no good." Presumably he was involved in criminal activities and tried to "hold back" on the "big guys." The woman was a hapless victim, someone who was at the wrong place at the wrong time. One woman remarked that the murdered woman had been shot in the eye, a sign that she had witnessed the execution of her friend and, consequently, had to be killed. Others believed that the woman had gotten what she deserved. One person expressed it in this fashion: "After all she knew what she was getting into because the guy she was living with was no good. What can you expect?" Some of her co-workers were shocked and saddened by the tragedy. They described their friend as a sweet and generous person who had the misfortune of being in love with a "hood." The murders remain unsolved.

Homicides are certainly not uncommon occurrences in the lives of the people of Monte Carmelo despite media reports. Indeed the Monte Carmelesi accept these acts of violence as either private matters that can be readily explained, rationalized, or as public acts of punishment. A bookie tries to hold back money from his boss, an Albanian and a Puerto Rican have an argument that ends in bloodshed — these are private acts. There are those killings that have more of a public character to them. Thieves who steal from the merchants and café owners are executed. A mugger who preys off the people in the community is caught by a group of young men who beat him mercilessly and leave him dying on the street. Many Monte Carmelesi would view such acts as just retribution. The punishment meted out by people in the community is certain and swift. In some instances, it can be fatal.

## NOTES

1. In September 1983, Figgie International, a Cleveland-based company, issued a

report in which some objective statistics and some objective observations were used to rate neighborhoods as safe or unsafe. Monte Carmelo was listed as one of the safest. Curiously, the police of the local precinct indicated that they did not have statistics on crime in the area (Wellisc 1983: sec. B, 1). See also English (1983: 5); James (1986: sec. B, 1); Moses (1985: 14).

# CHAPTER FOUR

# Family Profiles

The interpretation of family, *la familigia* or *parente*, may be relatively narrow or broad depending on the individual's awareness of
relationships. Indeed, for some, *la familigia* is a metaphor for the
entire ethnic enclave of Monte Carmelo. The basic structure,
however, is the nuclear unit consisting of parents and their offspring
or the limited extended family comprising a nuclear unit with some
additional relatives such as a grandparent or a sibling of the wife or
husband. In a number of instances an extended family may occupy
different levels in a house but share, to some extent, in common
chores and eat their principal meals together.

Beyond the nuclear unit and the extended family is the
kindred (*parentela*), a broad, bilateral kinship grouping composed
of blood ties, affinal ties (those based on marriage), and
*comare* and *compare* relationships. The latter, which are often formalized through church ritual, are frequently a blend of close
friendship and blood.

For most Monte Carmelesi the kindred extends beyond the
boundaries of the enclave. There are relatives living in other neighborhoods of the Bronx such as Pelham Bay, Morris Park, Throgs
Neck, Eastchester, Williamsbridge, and Country Club. In addition,
many have *parente* in Yonkers, Rockland County, and in communities located in New Jersey and Connecticut. Distance itself is not
necessarily a barrier to maintaining kindred ties. As one would
expect, kinspeople residing in nearby areas visit one another frequently. People may combine visits to *parente* in Monte Carmelo
with shopping in neighborhood stores.

Many Monte Carmelesi continue to maintain strong ties with their
relatives in Italy despite the thousands of miles separating them.
The phone call on Sunday — more so than a weekly or monthly
letter — is the important social channel of communication. The
letter, somehow, is too impersonal; it cannot convey the joy or the
sorrow, the laughter or the tears that accompany the flow of information about *parente* and *paesani*. To hear one's mother's voice
or a sister's account of the recent baptism of her youngest son

conjures up vivid images and recent memories of events when families were together.

Visits to and from Italy are not uncommon either. In a number of instances the visits lasted for months. Interestingly, some of those who do visit relatives for longer periods are young men and women. There are parents who are hoping that their sons and daughters will establish ties which will eventually lead to marriage. I know a number of cases where this did occur. Some young women pressure their parents to send them to Italy to visit a married sibling, preferably a sister, where they hope to escape the oppressive constraints of parents. Yet the members of one's *parentela*, whether in Apulia or Campania or Monte Carmelo, continue to scrutinize the behavior of its members.

One young woman who visited her parents' town became involved with a male cousin. It wasn't long before her parents were informed, and when she returned home she was vehemently upbraided. She was convinced that her parents were more concerned about "what my relatives must be saying and thinking than what's important to *me*." It was not really an issue of a cousin-cousin relationship, since in various parts of Italy cousin marriages are not uncommon. It was the flagrant dispaly of sexual interest — a flaunting of what is communally judged to be immoral behavior, in a town where *parente* and *paesani* are everywhere — that caused such a reaction. If the necessary steps had been taken to arrange a proper courtship, perhaps the relationship would not have created so much grief and embarrassment.

The ties of kinship are important linkages for individuals in their relationships with the broader social, economic, and political world and its institutional complexes which affect the daily lives of the Monte Carmelesi. Vittorio's nephew from Cosenza, Calabria, comes to live with his uncle's family while members of his kindred inquire about possible job opportunities for him. At the same time efforts are directed toward securing him an apartment in a well-kept, rent-controlled building where he and his young wife will live until they can save enough money to buy their own home. When people leave the community, they often follow kinspeople to other neighborhoods. Local patronage positions in community, educational, recreational, and social service organizations often depend on whether one's kin linkages and those of the community power brokers intermesh.

The linkages of blood, marriage, and the *comparaggio* (godparenthood) are further extended to *amici* (friends), a number of

whom may be referred to as *compare* and *paesani*. These also
include relatives and friends of *amici* and *paesani*.[1]
The bonds of kinship are not necessarily assurances of fidelity,
love, and, in general, cooperative behavior. On my block, for example, a brother and sister live just a few houses away from each other
but have not spoken to one another in years. The rift developed
sometime after their joint purchase of a two family home.
Apparently there were differences of opinion regarding the house
and its upkeep. No one seems to know precisely why the split
occurred, nor do they criticize either party. It's something that
concerns the individuals involved and no one else. The neighbors
have remained neutral.

Another example of a rift in the kindred involved Francesca's
family, one of the more prosperous families in Monte Carmelo. The
tensions erupted after the untimely death of her father at the age of
forty-five. His relatives immediately placed the blame for his death
on Francesca's mother. They accused her of "driving him too hard."
The mother owns a home, is part owner of another home, and has a
business as well. Furthermore, Francesca's maternal grandparents
own three buildings plus some land on Long Island. The maternal
side of Francesca's family has done well and her father's relatives
attribute part of their success to her "overworked" father. Francesca believes that there is a considerable amount of jealousy and
resentment on the part of her father's relatives. This might have
been engendered by the fact that they did not receive a share in his
estate. The acrimony and anger was felt in the funeral home itself.
During the wake, the seating arrangements were such that Francesca sat on the right side of her mother. Her father's relatives
challenged this and insisted that his oldest sister, not his oldest
daughter, should be seated in that position. Francesca emphasized
that their concern with appropriate protocol did not carry over into
the sharing of funeral expenses.

Despite the occasional severing of ties and petty squabbles, *la
familigia* continues to play an important role in the lives of the
Monte Carmelesi. Let us examine some of the families who live in
the community.

## FRANCESCA'S FAMILY

Francesca's mother's relatives are from a town near Naples. The
mother's family emigrated to the United States about thirty years

ago and secured a place on a main thoroughfare that forms the eastern border of Monte Carmelo. Her mother, her mother's brother, and her mother's parents worked in a garment factory. Francesca's father emigrated from a small town in Calabria about twenty-eight years ago and settled with his uncle's family in Brooklyn. Her parents met on a blind date and began meeting without her mother's parents' knowledge. Soon thereafter Francesca's grandparents became aware that their daughter was going out with a Calabrese and he was invited to the house to express his intentions. In August of 1959, Francesca's parents were married at our Lady of Mount Carmel Church and the newlyweds moved to Market Street. At about this time, her parents, her mother's brother, and her mother's parents purchased a three-family house on Market Street. Francesca's parents bought the top floor; her uncle, the middle floor; and her grandparents, the bottom floor. Some years later, Francesca's parents bought the building next door and moved in with their children.

I have listed below selected socio-cultural data on the various households that together comprise part of Francesca's *parentela*. The members of Francesca's household include:

Father: He died of a heart attack three years ago at the age of forty-five. He received three years of schooling in Italy but developed various technical and architectural skills on his own. He owned a construction business.

Mother: Francesca's mother is forty-five years old and owns a dry goods store. Like her husband, she came to the United States with very little formal education.

Francesca: She is twenty-two years old and a graduate of Mount St. Vincent College where she majored in sociology. She attended Our Lady of Mount Carmel elementary school and St. Catherine's Academy High School.

Sister: She is twenty-one years old and a junior at Pace College where she is a marketing major.

Sister: Francesca's youngest sister is nineteen and is in her first year at Fordham University.

Brother: The only brother is seventeen and he is in his junior year at Fordham Prep.

Like Francesca, her sisters and brother have gone to parochial elementary and high schools. As the oldest daughter, however, she was expected to prepare herself for the roles that all traditional

Italian women anticipated, wife and mother. At first her father resisted her efforts to go to college. Since Francesca did many of the housekeeping chores and had learned how to sew, knit, embroider, cook, and crochet, it was generally expected that she would marry soon after graduating from high school. In fact, her mother had tried to arrange a marriage for her but Francesca's father sided with his daughter and insisted that she be allowed to choose her husband.

While growing up, Francesca spent a considerable amount of time socializing and she had male as well as female friends. Most of her friends were from the neighborhood but many have moved out. She enjoyed going to high school dances.

As a young woman she attended mass at Our Lady of Mount Carmel every Sunday. Francesca was especially fond of the folk mass which was celebrated at 10 o'clock on Sunday morning. Many of the young people in Monte Carmelo participated in this mass which has been discontinued. Francesca, like her mother, rarely attends Sunday mass now, though she will go on holidays. Her father visited the church only on very special occasions such as his son's communion or a daughter's confirmation.

Francesca's father was active in sponsoring recreational activities in the community. He managed a soccer team and a number of the team's members served as pallbearers at his funeral. Her mother was active in fund-raising activities for the church.

Francesca's two younger sisters have evidenced less of the traditional behavior patterns than their older sibling. Her twenty-one-year-old sister has a boyfriend whose parents live in Boston. From time to time she drives to Boston with her boyfriend to visit them for a weekend. Her youngest sister often travels around with her college friends. These are the new ways, according to Francesca, which her parents had come to accept. But the demands of tradition still haunt Francesca. Unilke her sisters who wore black only for the wake and funeral of their father, she continued in mourning clothes for seven months. Francesca has grown up in two worlds. The world of her parents and grandparents, where a woman's role was clearly defined, comprised the first, and perhaps, most enduring. Friends, the college experience, and the media, have presented her with yet another world where options and choices conflict with the expectations of parents and grandparents. Francesca, unlike her younger siblings, has reluctantly embraced the more traditionalist orientations.

From an economic perspective, Francesca's household is a relatively comfortable one. Annual household income, i.e., reported income, is in excess of $30,000. Assets in the form of real estate holdings are probably about $100,000–$150,000.

The real estate holdings of her maternal grandparents, both of whom are in their seventies, are probably worth more than $400,000. Francesca's mother and maternal uncle stand to inherit the lion's share of the property. And although Francesca's father's death has cut off income from the household, her mother received a substantial amount of money from her husband's insurance policy.

A brief description of the other households that constitute Francesca's *parentela* follows. Most of these kinspeople live on the same street. Her mother's brother's household is composed of:

Uncle: He is forty-nine years old and completed five years of school. He owns a grocery store.

Aunt: Forty-four years old and a high school graduate, she works with her husband in the grocery store.

Female cousin: Francesca's twenty-one-year-old cousin is a graduate of a local parochial high school. She is married to an automobile mechanic.

Female cousin: She is fifteen years old and attends a local public high school.

Male cousin: He is nine and a student at a local public elementary school.

In Francesca's mother's brother's household the combined income and assets are in excess of $125,000.

The following are the members of Francesca's father's oldest sister's household:

Aunt: She is fifty, had five years of schooling, and works as a seamstress in her home.

Uncle: He is sixty years old and works as a barber.

Male Cousin: He is a twenty-six-year-old hairstylist. After getting married, he and his wife, a neighborhood girl, left Monte Carmelo and moved to nearby Pelham Parkway.

Male cousin: A twenty-four-year-old computer specialist, he received an associate degree from a technical school.

Female cousin: She is twenty-two years old and has an elementary school education. In addition to working for an insurance company, she has numerous household responsibilities. Her parents carefully supervise her and hope to match her up with a young man from Italy.

Male cousin: He is seventeen years old and a high school junior. Like many young people in Monte Carmelo, he does not attend the local public high school, preferring to go to Columbus High School where there is a sizable Italian-American student population. He often acts as a father surrogate for his twenty-two-year-old sister. He works part-time in a supermarket.

The household income is $35,000–$40,000. With the exception of the married son who no longer lives in the household, the children give half their salaries to their parents.

Included in Francesca's father's brother's household are:

Uncle: Two years younger than Francesca's father, he, like his older brother did, makes his living in the construction business. He completed five years of schooling.

Aunt: She is forty-three years old and a homemaker.

Male cousin: Deceased.

Male cousin: He is fifteen years old and attends a parochial high school.

Male counsin: He attends the local parochial elementary school and is thirteen years old.

Female cousin: She is ten years old and attends the same school as her thirteen-year-old brother.

Francesca's uncle and aunt own their own home which is the building next to that of Francesca's family. The annual household income is approximately $20,000.

In Francesca's father's youngest sister's household, the members are:

Aunt: She is thirty-nine years old, a high school graduate, and works as a seamstress. Because of her exceptional skills in her work, she is considered a "head seamstress."

Uncle: He is forty-seven years old and works as a welder.

Cousins: Two males, thirteen and nine years old, and one female, seven years old, attend a parochial elementary school situated outside of the neighborhood.

The family has purchased a home on a relatively small, quiet street bordering on a university campus. Francesca's paternal grandparents, who are in their seventies, live with their youngest daughter.

In analyzing a significant segment of Francesca's *parentela*, one notes that she has thirty relatives living in six separate domiciles, though one could include in Francesca's household her maternal grandparents who live next door (or, perhaps, vice versa) since the two units often function as one. Most of these relatives live on the same block and the others live merely a few blocks away. The average household consists of five people and household income varies from $20,000 to $50,000 and more. In a number of instances household assets exceed $125,000. These figures, in my judgment, are quite conservative and more than likely underrepresent actual earnings from wages, rentals, and businesses. Similarly, they do not reflect the true, current value of real estate property. However one interprets the figures, there is little doubt that Francesca's maternal relatives are more prosperous than her paternal side of the *parentela*.

These economic differences may have engendered some jealousy on the part of her father's relatives. Perhaps bitterness would be a more appropriate expression of their reaction to the attitude of Francesca's mother and her family toward Francesca's father who was, after all, a son and a brother to them. Here, of course, I am referring to his parents and siblings who pointed an accusatory finger at Francesca's mother for driving her husband so hard. The meaning was quite clear. He had given his all, so his family prospered. The rancor and accusations seemed to revolve around the hoary issue of a person's loyalty to one's old family (parents and siblings) or to one's new family (wife and children).[2] The very least his parents and siblings expected was a modest share of his inheritance. They received nothing; his wife everything.

The wake of Francesca's father became the setting for a reenactment of the intra-kindred squabble, a conflict of loyalties as played out by one's *familigia*. Francesca's grandmother had to be restrained a she attempted to throw herself on her son's coffin. Her tears and mournful sounds reflected the loss of a beloved and loving son, a son that she nursed, fussed over, and raised to be a hard worker. Her expression of sorrow was a reminder of the enduring bond between mother and offspring. "No bond is stronger," was the message conveyed in the dramatic outburst in front of Francesca's father's coffin. And as was noted above, Francesca's alleged usurpation of her father's oldest sister's seating position was a clear signal that the break within the kindred had widened.

One discerns intra-ethnic variations in Francesca's *parentela*, with a sizeable segment reflecting a more Italian orientation. This seems to be true of Francesca herself, though her younger siblings, especially her sisters, are exhibiting "American ways," according to their grandmother. There are other families in Monte Carmelo where "Italian ways" are emphasized: within the household, within the kindred, in the café, at work in a local garment factory, in some of the shops, and with friends.

## JOE'S FAMILY

Joe and his father live in an apartment building which contains twenty-three other households, one of which consists of a maternal aunt and cousins. Like many families in Monte Carmelo they pay a relatively low rent, less than $200 per month. Joe's parents are divorced. His mother has since remarried and has moved out of the neighborhood.

There are two members in Joe's household:

Father: Born in the neighborhood, he is forty-eight years old and completed ten years of schooling. He works as a painter at a city college. Father and son communicate only in English. He has no relatives living in the neighborhood. One sister lives in the Bronx; she is divorced and has no children. Another sister lives on Long Island and has two children, both of whom are college graduates. The daughter is married and lives near the mother. The son lives with his parents. Joe's father also has a brother who moved to Canada where he secured a position as a teacher.

Joe: He is twenty-one years old and a junior at one of the City University senior colleges. As a youngster, Joe attended the local parochial school and went on to graduate from a vocational high school located in the neighborhood. Since the age of thirteen, Joe has had a variety of part-time jobs. The most recent one is at a video store.

The combined father and son income is about $25,000 a year.

Joe spent more time in Monte Carmelo when he was younger. Now school and work keep him out of the neighborhood for long periods of time. He indicated that his neighborhood peer group consists of Italian-Americans. At work he socialized with friends of various ethnic backgrounds. His girlfriend is Puerto Rican. Joe's cousins and his maternal aunts are encouraging him to marry an Italian-American girl. This is their way of expressing their disapproval of his relationship with a Puerto Rican woman. Even his friends in the community are pressuring him to "break up with her." Joe's father, however, has been supportive. In fact, Joe's father is seeing a Cuban woman and is seriously considering marrying her.

Joe enjoys dancing, "picking up girls," drinking, and playing softball. It appears that when a young man becomes "serious" with a woman, his ties with the peer group, which often consist in part of kin, become somewhat attenuated. Joe frequently "hung-out" with two of his male cousins, both of whom became "serious" with neighborhood girls. He sees less of his cousins now than before. Joe made a point of stressing that not one of his maternal cousins who live in the community has completed high school. He is the only member of his neighborhood kindred to seek a college education.

Marriage, for Joe, is something that may happen later in life. Perhpas his parents' unsuccessful marriage has jaundiced his perception of married life. He refused to answer questions about his mother, and I quickly realized the less said the better. However, Joe was quite clear about his feelings that once married, the spouses should be faithful to one another. Even in a "serious relationship," one which he describes as extending beyond a few months, each should be true to the other. In the meantime, Joe wants to have time to "fool around."

Joe and his kin exemplify the more American-oriented Italian-Americans of Monte Carmelo. The life style, especially as it is manifested in the language spoken at home and with kinspeople and friends, friendship ties with non-Italian-Americans both inside and outside the community, recreational interests, hang-out sites, club membership in the community, and "serious" dating and eventual marriage with someone from another ethnic group, is shared by Joe and others in Monte Carmelo.

Joe's family's roots in the neighborhood extend back more than fifty years. In that time span many people have left, others have stayed, and still others have come to replace those who left. Joe, his father, and his maternal kindred have adapted to changing conditions and changing times. They, and others like them, have become a subgroup of the Italian-American population in Monte Carmelo.

## MARIO'S FAMILY

Despite the large exodus of Italian-Americans from the community during the late 1960s and the 1970s, there were still families emigrating from Italy and settling in Monte Carmelo. Mario's family is one such family.

The following people comprise Mario's household:

Father: A forty four-year-old construction worker who completed eight years of schooling, he emigrated from Flumieri (in the Naples vicinity) in 1973 and took up residence with a brother who lived in Monte Carmelo. It wasn't long before he obtained a position with a construction company. In 1974 he returned to Flumieri in order to bring his family over. He moved them into a two-bedroom apartment in Monte Carmelo which was renting for $140 per month. When they moved out of Monte Carmelo six years later to a nearby residential neighborhood, the rent had gone up to a mere $170 a month.

Mario's father joined a hometown association consisting of men who had emigrated from Potenza. He enjoys playing cards and *bocce* (bowling-type game) with his association brothers, and occasionally goes to soccer matches. Mario's parents frequently go out together to visit relatives or to attend mass.

Mother: She is a year older than her husband, has completed the second grade of elementary school, and works as a seamstress. Like her husband, she was born in Flumieri.

Mario's mother is the most religious member of the household. She has a special devotion to St. Anthony and keeps a statue of the saint in front of the house. In addition to her traditional Catholic beliefs and practices, she holds to some folk beliefs and remedies. For her, *mal occhio* continues to afflict people. She and others tend to view this particular condition as a form of witchcraft. Poor health, an accident, a string of bad luck, or perhaps something as commonplace as a headache — all of these things and other misfortunes as well — are the telltale signs that the hapless victims are suffering the woes of the evil eye. Maybe an envious neighbor, friend, *paesano*, or even a relative, has unleased an evil force, willingly or otherwise, which undermines the well-being of the person. The most effective method in dealing with the probability of being afflicted is to use the appropriate prophylactic device — an amulet shaped in the form of horns. Failing that, and in the event that you encounter someone whom you suspect to be harboring the evil eye, one simply extends one's index finger and pinky finger towards the person. This is done in a surreptitious manner to avoid any recriminations.

Mario: The oldest of six children, five boys and one girl, Mario is twenty two years old and a senior at one of the City Univesity's four-year colleges where he is majoring in business management. When he arrived from Italy at the age of fifteen, he was placed in the eighth grade at the local junior high school. Soon thereafter, he was shifted to the seventh grade, mainly because of language difficulties. Ultimately, Mario convinced the school officials that he was capable of doing work well above his grade level. As a result, he was assigned to a ninth-grade gifted class. All of the grade changes took place within the first year of his arrival from Flumieri. After graduating from junior high school, Mario attended the local high school for barely two weeks before transferring to Columbus High School. Mario wangled the transfer by indicating that he was interested in registering for Latin courses which were not offered at his local high school but were being given at Columbus. The local high school had become less attractive to neighborhood residents because the ethnic composition of the student body began to reflect, in a rather striking way, the population diversity of the general area. The bitter confrontations of the late sixties and early seventies had not been easily forgotten. Mario and his family emigrated to Monte Carmelo soon after the worst of the violence had subsided. Memories of the violence, however, were still vivid in the minds of the people, both young and old, many of whom viewed the local high school as a symbol of neighborhood deterioration. As the number of Black and Puerto Rican students increased, there was a corresponding decrease in the enrollment of Italian-Americans, a number of whom managed to get into Columbus; others entered parochial high schools.

While attending high school, Mario had little time for school clubs since he often held part-time jobs. His peer group was somewhat mixed, consisting of both sexes and including Italian-oriented and American-oriented Italian-Americans. He socialized with school friends as well as neighborhood friends. One of the group became Mario's "steady girlfriend" for four years. A breakup occurred when Mario discovered that she had dated his best friend, a young man from the neighborhood. Despite her pleas for forgiveness, Mario refused to continue the relationship. He felt doubly betrayed.

For Mario, a traditional Italian woman would make the ideal wife. It is important that she be a virgin and a good mother to their children. In the meantime, he prefers to go out with "worldly" women for short periods of time. "There's time enough for marriage and children."

Mario, like a number of other Italian-oriented Italian-Americans, is an avid soccer player as well as a soccer fan. He carefully follows the progress of the more popular soccer teams of Italy. While living in Monte Carmelo, he was a member of one of the three adult soccer clubs.

Mario was also a member of the Mount Carmel Catholic Club, a group of boys and girls of high school age who regularly met on Friday evenings for Bible classes and social activities. Mario became less involved in church functions in subsequent years. Today he rarely attends mass, though he may make an effort to go on Christmas and Easter.

Brother: He is a twenty-year-old computer science major at a senior college of CUNY. He attended the local junior high school and, unlike his older brother, completed the years of high school at North Street High, the neighborhood school. As is generally the case for young Italian-American men and women, Mario's brother holds a part-time position in order to earn money for his personal needs. He is not very active in community organizations and rarely attends church.

Sister: Mario's only sister, age nineteen, attends Fordham University. She intends to study law after earning her undergraduate degree. Her earlier education included the neighborhood Catholic elementary school and interestingly, North Street High. Unlike Mario who was determined to find a way to transfer to an out-of-district high school, his sister was encouraged to stay in the neighborhood for her high school education. Despite the changing ethnic composition of North Street High, it appeared less threatening for a girl than for a boy. Moreover, the trip to an out-of-neighborhood high school may be viewed as more dangerous for a girl, not only in terms of possible physical and psychological harm but, also, in yet another sense: girls travelling outside of the protective screen of their neighborhood are less likely to conform to the behavior expectations of parents and kin. Even the selection of a college is predicated on the assumption that a young woman, more so than a young man, should be as close to home as possible. Mario's sister, like a number of young women in Monte Carmelo, find colleges and universities like Fordham, Lehman, Iona, and Mercy, convenient neighborhood or near-neighborhood schools. Attending these institutions would be more acceptable to their parents than commuting long distances or, worse still, living away from home. One young woman who is a few years older than Mario's sister and a graduate of Fordham expressed the dilemma that seems to bother others as well: "I really wanted to go away to college because I knew it would have been a good experience for me; but I understood that this would not be acceptable to my parents." She, Mario's sister, and others recognize the parameters of traditional expectations.

During the six years that she lived in Monte Carmelo, Mario's sister's peer group consisted of school friends from the neighborhood. She worked part-time, attended church regularly, and occasionally managed to break away from the claustrophobic scrutiny of parents, older sibling, and neighbors.

Mario has three other male siblings, ages eleven, thirteen, and sixteen. While living in Monte Carmelo, the three attended the local schools and established ties with the more American-oriented Italian-Americans. Like their older brother, they rarely go to church. According to Mario, his three youngest brothers speak a "broken Italian" to their parents and English to their siblings. The older siblings, on the other hand, speak a more fluent Italian and converse in the language not only with their parents but with one another and with friends and relatives as well.

The household income is approximately $33,000 per year. Mario's parents pay for the general household expenditures. The children who work buy their own clothing and use their own earnings for educational and recreational expenses. They make no contributions to the maintenance of the household unless the parents are "short" of money.

A few years ago Mario's family purchased a home near Eastchester Road and Mace Avenue in the Bronx. The area is predominantly residential and many of the homeowners are Italian-Americans. The top floor of the house has been converted into an apartment which has been rented out. This makes the mortgage payment of $580 a month less of a hardship. When the family began looking for a home they consulted friends and *paesani*. It wasn't long before a *paesano* apprised them of a "nice house" for sale in a "good neighborhood." Within seven years, Mario and his family emigrated from Italy, settled in Monte Carmelo and, after saving for a down payment, bought a home in a relatively quiet "middle-class" neighborhood in the Bronx.

Mario's family is certainly not unique nor is it particularly atypical in its residential mobility. There have been others, some of whom have moved out as far back as the 1920s and for the very same reasons: a better dwelling; less congestion; and a parcel of land, however small. The flow of people into and out of Monte Carmelo dates back to the early decades of this century. Overall, more people settled in the community than left. Nevertheless, there were those, like Mario and his family, who rented apartments for a few years and sometimes longer, and then went on to newly purchased homes or more spacious apartments in other areas of the Bronx and elsewhere in the general metropolitan region. Monte Carmelo was merely a stopping point, an interlude, for a number of Italian-Americans.

## MARY'S FAMILY

Father: He was born in Avellino (near Naples) in 1893 and was sent to school for three years. He married a *paesana* and within a few years he emigrated to Bridgeport, Connecticut, leaving his daughter and pregnant wife behind. Eight years later, Mary's mother and two older sisters joined her father in Bridgeport.

Mary's father earned his living as a painter. While in Bridgeport, he worked under a contract arrangement which, among other things, involved painting the inside of churches. As the family moved from one state to another and from one community to another, her father continued supporting the family as a painter. He died in 1974 at the age of eighty-one.

Mother: Also born in Avellino, Mary's mother was five years older than her father and had completed eights years of schooling. After marrying and emigrating to the United States she took in sewing to augment her husband's income. She died in 1967 at the age of seventy-nine.

Sister: Mary's oldest sister, seventy-three, was born in Avellino and, with her mother and six-year-old sister, emigrated to the United States when she was eleven years old. She had completed five years of elementary school and, like her mother, worked as a seamstress. At the age of nineteen she married an Italian-American who earned his living as a pushcart peddler in East Harlem. Subsequently, she and her husband opened a business in that neighborhood.

Mary's sister has five children, three sons and two daughters. All are high school graduates and four of the five are married and own their own homes in the Throg's Neck section of the Bronx. Mary's sister lives with her unmarried daughter in East Harlem.

Sister: She was born in Avellino sixty-eight years ago. After emigrating to the United States, she was enrolled in an elementary
school and was taken out by her parents after the seventh grade, at
which time she began honing her sewing skills. Like her mother and
older sister, she became a seamstress. At eighteen she married an
Italian-American and thereafter gave birth to her only child, a
daughter. Her first marriage ended in a divorce, but she remarried.
Her daughter has been married and divorced twice. She has three
children and two grandchildren.

Mary's sister and her sister's second husband currently live in
lower Westchester County.

Mary: She was born in Bridgeport, Connecticut in 1919. In 1920,
the family moved to Edgewater, New Jersey. When Mary was three
years old, the family settled in East Harlem. She vividly recalls the
poverty she and her family endured during the early years of her
life. Her father worked intermittently and the family depended on
credit extended by the merchants in the neighborhood.

Mary's education in East Harlem included elementary school and
junior high. Although she never completed high school, she managed to earn her high school equivalency diploma at the age of
fifty-four. She later enrolled in a community college and accumu-
lated thirty-four credits.

In her early years in East Harlem, her play group consisted of
both boys and girls, including a younger sister. At the age of seven,
she joined the choir at Holy Rosary Church on 119th Street. Three
years later she became an "Aspirant" in Our Lady Sodality at the
same church. In another three years she became a "Junior," and by
sixteen a "Senior."

Although Mary was given household responsibilities by the age of
nine, she managed to engage in outdoor street and park sports,
including stoopball and stickball, both of which she played with
boys. She also enjoyed playing basketball with the church team.
When she reached the age of thirteen, her parents would no longer
allow her to play with boys; instead, she was sent to sewing classes
which were taught by nuns at a settlement house. Despite her
parents pronouncement, Mary continued to associate with boys,
though in a surreptitious and carefully planned way. A group of
boys and girls would agree to meet at the beach or in front of a
movie house. Mary would tell her parents that she was going to
Orchard Beach or the Loews Theatre with her girlfriends. Having

her younger sister along would make the story more credible. By the age of fifteen she was "going steady." This was short-lived because the family moved to 170th Street and 3rd Aveenue. Within a year she fell in love with a handsome seventeen-year-old Italian-American from her new neighborhood. They began "going steady," and when Mary was eighteen the engagement was formalized by an exchange of rings and a recognition by the two families of the intention of marriage. Although Mary's two older sisters were under constant parental scrutiny, she was able to go out wih her boyfriend unescorted.

In 1938, Mary's family moved to Monte Carmelo, their sixth move in nineteen years. Still, Mary continued to attend mass at her old parish church in East Harlem, a practice she followed after moving to 170th Street. And she continued singing in the choir at the Church of the Holy Rosary, something that she had so enjoyed doing since the age of seven. When she married at age twenty-one, she returned to East Harlem and the church of her youth for the wedding ritual. Mary described the wedding reception as the traditional "football wedding." These were not catered and were relatively inexpensive receptions compared to today's elaborate $20,000 wedding celebrations. The "football wedding reception" consisted of sandwiches: salami, provolone, prosciutto, capicola, ham, American cheese, etc.; drinks, including beer, sodas, and wine; and Italian cookies and confetti (Italian candy). Friends were invited of course, but it was, above all, a family affair. All family members, from the very old to the very young, close and distant relatives, were invited. For many Italian-Americans, today's catered and exhorbitantly expensive wedding receptions often exclude young relatives other than siblings and youngsters in the bridal party. For Mary, the "football wedding" had more meaning since it included children and teenagers and it was much more family oriented. According to Mary, her husband paid for the church ceremony, the reception, and the rental of her wedding gown.

Mary's early working experiences included employment in a variety of factories. After marriage her husband insisted that she quit her job and devote all of her energies to homemaking activities. Actually, Mary enjoyed the role. At last she felt she could do things her way. The yoke of parents and older siblings was finally severed. An apartment of her own, a husband, and, hopefully, within a year or two, a child; these were the important pieces that for Mary made the whole woman. And this is what Mary had been anticipating since she began going steady at the age of fifteen.

Mary described her husband as someone who was not unwilling to help with household chores, even during the early years of their marriage. She also characterized him as the sort of person who was "involved" with the community and was active in church organizations. He was a member of the Holy Name Society and headed the Usher's Society. In addition, he served as a volunteer worker at church bazaars and at bingo.[3] His other church-related activities included the collection of donations for the parochial school, canvassing for Catholic Charities, and chairing sessions of the Christian Family Movement which was an educational and social forum for married couples in the partish.

Both Mary and her husband arranged for the twenty-fifth and fiftieth wedding anniversary celebrations for members of the church. This involved sending invitations and arranging for a reception. Mary was a member of St. Ann's Sodality, serving as an instructor of initiants and as Treasurer. Because of her service to the association, Mary was the recipient of the Sodality Gold Pin which was given to her by Cardinal Spellman. Years later her daughter was to receive the same award. This was the first time in the history of the diocese that a mother and daughter had received such an honor.

Mary's husband suffered a cerebral hemorrhage at the age of forty-eight. Three years later he had a heart attack. His second heart attack at fifty-six was fatal. Mary has never remarried. For the past fourteen years she has been earning a living as a paraprofessional in a neighborhood elementary school. Her income is approximately $11,000 a year.

Daughter: She is thirty-nine years old, a high school graduate, and the mother of two boys, ages seventeen and thirteen. The son-in-law is an Italian-oriented Italian-American who speaks very little English. Mary's daughter, on the other hand, speaks very little Italian. After the wedding the couple moved to 174th Street and Parkchester Avenue in the Bronx. Five years later the family moved to a new house in Ronkonkoma, Long Island. The son-in-law is a machinist by trade and holds two jobs.

Daughter: She is a thirty-three year old college graduate who teaches at a local elementary school. Her husband, an Irish-American, is a computer operator. The daughter, her fourteen-year-old son, and her husband live in a nearby Bronx neighborhood.

Son: He is thirty-one years old, a high school graduate and married to an Italian-American and Irish-American woman. They have two children and presently live in Sloatsburg, New York. He works for a telephone company and his wife, a college graduate, worked for eight years to save money to buy a home. She has since quit her job to be a "full-time" mother and homemaker. Son: The youngest of Mary's children, he is twenty-seven years old and a high school graduate. Mary describes him as a "sickly boy." He works as a maintenance person at Mt. Vernon Hospital. He married an Italian-American woman and they have on child. The family lives in Mt. Vernon (Westchester County).

Like many older residents of Monte Carmelo, Mary raised her children in the neighborhood and stayed on as each of them married and moved out. Now she is a widow who lives alone but continues to lead an active life. Her children and their families visit on holidays. She sees her thirty-three-year-old daughter most often, since she lives in a nearby neighborhood. And from time to time Mary visits her daughter in Ronkonkoma or her son in Sloatsburg for a few weeks. On Palm Sunday her children and grandchildren gather at her house. A Christmas Eve get–together is held at either one of her children's homes, her husband sister's home, or her youngest sister's home. Actually, Mary prefers to have her weekends without her children and grandchildren. Saturday, for her, is cleaning day and she looks forward to going out with a friend, also a widow, on Sunday.

Sister: She is fifty-nine years old and married to an Italian-American who works for the New York City Transit Authority. They have four children. Although she never completed high school, she earned a High School Equivalency Diploma. The family lives in New Jersey.

Sister: Mary's youngest sibling is fifty years old and a graduate of Washington Irving High School. She currently works for a telephone company. Her husband, an Italian, worked as a dress cutter before he and his wife opened up their own dress cutting business in upper Manhattan. Within a short time, they established a second one just a few blocks away. Business was picking up considerably and her husband purchased two garment factories in Colombia, South America and another factory in Woodside, Queens. She and her husband purchased a spacious home in Port Chester, New York, and had a live-in maid. Since those halcyon days of success and fortune, she and her husband have separated. Now Mary's sister and her nineteen-year-old niece, a college student, reside in a comfortable condominium in Yonkers.

In addition to her siblings, children, and grandchildren, all of whom live outside the neighborhood, Mary has other relatives including an aunt (mother's sister) in Patterson, New Jersey; a cousin in Flushing, Queens; and another in Rosedale, Queens. She regularly calls her aunt in Patterson, but rarely calls her cousins.

Mary is the last of her family in Monte Carmelo. For her it is home, a home that she shared with family and friends for more than forty years.

## CARLA'S FAMILY

Mother: She emigrated from Salerno at the age of fifteen. She, her father, and four siblings settled with relatives in Buenos Aires, Argentina. Five years later they left Argentina for the United States. After living in East Harlem for several years, the family moved to Monte Carmelo, Carla's mother completed nine years of education before being taken out of school by her father. Carla's grandmother had died and her mother had to assume household responsibilities. Even after her marriage at the age of twenty-two, she continued in her role as the principal homemaker for her father, in addition to her normal responsibilities as wife and mother.

Carla described her mother as an intensely religious person, who heard mass every day and joined church associations. Every Monday evening for the prescribed period of time she participated in the novena offered in honor of the Immaculate Conception. She was also, according to Carla, devoted to her family. Her home was the gathering place for the family whether it be for holiday celebrations, the baptism of a grandchild, or for a Sunday *pranzo* (dinner). Carla's mother died in 1955 at the age of sixty-one.

Father: At the age of fourteen he was an emigrant from Abruzzi who had made the voyage alone to join his cousins who were living in East Harlem. When he emigrated, he had already completed eight years of education in Italy. His only exposure to schooling in the United States was for a brief period in an adult education program. He became an apprentice construction worker who, through years of hard labor, moved up to a foreman's position.

Like his wife, he was active in church affairs and attended mass every Sunday. He insisted that the children go as well. Carla described her father's recreational activities as visiting with male friends, card playing, playing *bocce* and going to the movies with his wife.

A few years after his wife's death, Carla's father married a woman from the neighborhood. At first Carla was quite upset, but gradually she came to accept the marriage, recognizing that her mother "did everything for him and he needed someone to take her place."

Carla's stepmother and mother had been good friends. It was only fitting that at the death of her father in 1975, at the age of eighty-six, Carla's stepmother would express her feelings in a tender and moving way. They were at the cemetary and Carla's father was to be buried next to her mother. It was then that Carla's stepmother stated in a soft and tearful voice that she was returning to her dear friend the husband that was rightfully hers.

Brother: Carla's oldest brother is a sixty-six-year-old bachelor who works as an engineer at the Sperry Company. He attended neighborhood public schools, served as a medic in World War II, and completed college at Manhattan after his discharge from the army. He lives with an unmarried sister and a bachelor brother in Monte Carmelo. According to Carla he has many friends, travels a great deal, and hears mass on special holidays.

Brother: He is sixty-three years old and works as a bridge operator for the City of New York. Unlike his older brother, his education ended with a high school diploma. For the past twenty-two years, he, his wife, and six children have been living in the Throgs Neck section of the Bronx. Still, Carla's family and her brother's family frequently visit one another.

Sister: She is sixty-two years old, unmarried, and a high school graduate who attended a secretarial school for a period of time. Carla describes her as the "caretaker" for the two brothers living with her. She attends mass regularly at Our Lady of Monte Carmelo and continues to maintain ties with old friends who no longer live in the community.

Brother: The youngest of her three brothers, he is fifty-eight years old and works in the produce department of a large supermarket. Carla describes her brother as "very Italian." He is a member of a social club in Monte Carmelo and is a regular at Sunday mass. Still, he often travels outside the community not only to commute to work but to visit friends and for other types of recreation.

Carla: Often referred to as the "baby" of the family, she is in her early fifties. Like her siblings before her, she attended the neighborhood public schools and received her high school diploma from North Side High. Some time late she enrolled for a few courses at Mercy College.

Carla recalled that her family responsibilities began at about the age of ten, whereas her older sisters were given household chores when they were seven or eight years old. Carla's major duty was to pick up daily food items in the local stores. And although she often played with her friends in the street and on the sidewalk, she was required to be within "calling distance."

Visiting relatives and friends were always rather special occasions for Carla and her siblings who often anticipated receiving candies or sweets of some sort. Yet none of them dared take a piece of candy or accept a slice of cake unless their mother nodded her approval. Children who simply grabbed for the food were considered ill-mannered and poorly raised. Ostensibly, these would seem to be the impressions that the parents would not want their children to convey. What would be more devastating to the parents would be if the hosts were to suspect that the children were normally deprived of these special treats at home. Moreover, these were expensive and nonessential items and, consequently, were in scarce supply. Therefore, it was incumbent on the family, especially on the children who might become somewhat overzealous in reaching for the sweets, to exercise restraint. Mothers carefully trained their children to respond in a controlled manner to their visual clues. For Carla and her siblings, their mother's gentle nod was the welcome sign that one could accept the offer of candy or cake. Each took a piece, hoping for yet another nod if another offer were to be made.

In addition to visiting relatives and friends, Carla's family often went to the zoo on Sundays.

Although the father was the titular head of the family, Carla's mother was the disciplinarian whose ready hand would slap a disrespectful or disobedient child. Carla had no recollection of ever being physically punished by her father who was as close to her as her mother.

As a young teenager, her friendship network extended beyong the confines of her neighborhood block to classmates in both junior high and high school. Her parent's anxieties did not dissuade Carla from maintaining ties with a peer group consisting of males and females. Her future husband was one of the young men from the group. Her recreational activities were fairly varied: church dances, Sunday afternoon movies, skating, reading, listening to the radio, crocheting, and stamp collecting. Sundays were often family days and all the children were required to be at the table for the Sunday afternoon *pranzo* and the Sunday evening snack. It was also expected that the family share weekday suppers together.

Carla was very involved in school activities and organizations. She served as her class president for the tenth, eleventh, and twelveth grades and was an active member of the Italian Club. When she was in her junior year of high school, Carla began "going steady." After graduating from North Street High, Carla and her boyfriend became *fidanzarsi*, a formally engaged couple. Her parents hosted an engagement party in their home where the future groom presented Carla with an engagement ring selected by his mother.

The *fidanzamento* lasted for a period of eighteen months. The engaged couple then celebrated their marriage at Our Lady of Mount Carmel Church. The groom's sister served as maid of honor and his brother as best man. One of Carla's sisters, a cousin, and two of her girlfriends were the bridesmaids. A niece and nephew served as ring bearers. The wedding reception, the "football type," was held in a hall in Manhattan. Carla and her husband travelled to Arizona for their honeymoon.

Through the years, Carla developed a strong commitment to Catholicism. She often attends mass and special novenas. As a young woman, she was a member of the Blessed Mother Society. In addition to her religious activities, Carla was a member of the now defunct Republican Club and, in spite of its demise, she continues to be an active voice in community affairs.

During their married life, Carla and her husband have enjoyed going to dinner-dances, some of which were sponsored by local associations. In addition, she often gets together with friends from her high school days, a number of whom still live in Monte Carmelo.

For Carla, the neighborhood is no longer what it used to be. Although she still loves the community, she feels that she may have to move out soon. Because of her fears, she confines herself to certain parts of Monte Carmelo — areas of heavier Italian-American concentrations. She made a point of stating that the apartments in her building are all occupied by Italian-Americans.

For the past twelve years, Carla has been working as a paraprofessional in a local public elementary school. With three members of the household working, the combined annual income is over

$50,000. The apartment rents for $225 per month.

Husband: Raised in Monte Carmelo, he is fifty-six years old, and a graduate of Manhattan Aviation High School. He holds a managerial level position with a major airline.

Son: Thirty-three years old, he attended the local public elementary and junior high schools. He is a graduate of the Bronx High School of Science and the City College of New York where he majored in education. Presently he works in the administration division of Yeshiva University. He and his wife, an Italian-American, live in a nearby neighborhood and, according to Carla, visit twice a week — Friday evenings and Sundays — and on holidays.

Daughter: Carla's thirty-two-year-old daughter completed twelve years of education in the local public schools. She married a young man from the neighborhood who currently works for the post office. She, her husband, and her two children live next door to her older brother and, like her brother's family, they frequently return to the old neighborhood to visit.

Son: Carla's youngest son, thirty-one, attended the local public schools from kindergarten through high school. He left home to attend college in West Virginia where he met his wife. Presently he is employed by a pharmaceutical company and is separated from his wife. They have no children. Carla's son continues to maintain close ties with his parents and siblings.

Daughter: The youngest of Carla's children is twenty-five years old, single, and lives with her parents. Her education ended with a high school diploma from a neighborhood vocational high school. She works as a secretary in a savings bank.

The members of Carla's family, like the overwhelming majority of Italian-Americans, view themselves a Catholics and maintain ritual ties with the church in some form or other. All have been baptized, have received their first communion, have been confirmed, and have been married in the church. In addition, most go to church regularly and just about all of them make a special effort to attend mass on Palm Sunday, Easter, and Christmas. All of the grandchildren have been baptized, and it is expected that they will follow the religious traditions of their parents and grandparents by receiving the Church sacraments throughout the course of their lives.

The last time I had seen Carla was on a pleasant Sunday afternoon in July, the first Sunday of the Mount Carmel feast. People were walking down Main Street, some stopping at booths to buy pepper and sausage sandwiches or calzones. Others were in cafés and clubs listening to the play-by-play description of the world championship soccer game between Italy and West Germany. Suddenly, the community erupted into a frenzy of celebration. Carla, her husband, and their daughter were part of a huge outpouring of people — some coming from their homes and others from clubs, cafés, and stores — all gathering on Main Street and Bishop Perone Square. The Monte Carmelesi were celebrating the Italian soccer victory over West Germany which gave the Italian team the World Cup. Carla was no less jubilant than the most avid Italian-American soccer fan. She, like so many others, was caught up in the collective display of ethnic pride. It was a joyous moment.

Four months later Carla was dead. She had succumbed to cancer that she thought had been cured. Her last months were a tragic testimony to the hopelessness and despair which often afflict the terminally ill. She could scarcely fight back the tears when her friends came to visit. She desperately wanted to live, to be part of the lives of her children and grandchildren, to share in the learning experiences of the school children whom she so loved. Ultimately she turned to God for the strength to die.

Soon after Carla's death, her husband married a woman that a number of people suspected was his mistress of long standing. He and his new wife immediately left Monte Carmelo for the suburbs of New Jersey.


## COMPARATIVE DATA ON FAMILY INCOMES AND OCCUPATIONS OF THE MAJOR ETHNIC-RACIAL CATEGORIES IN MONTE CARMELO[4]

Since approximately 72 percent of the White persons listed in those census tracts which correspond to the traditional village of Monte Carmelo are Italian-Americans, the 1980 census figures listing household incomes and occupations provide some indication of the socio-economic status of the Italian-Americans in the community. This information, along with selected data on families of Spanish Origin (primarily Puerto Rican) and Blacks, provides a comparative framework for noting similarities and differences within a neighborhood which had been at one time an almost exclusively Italian-American community.

Table 1. Income Distribution of White Households in Monte Carmelo, 1979

| Income | Number of Households |
|---|---|
| Less than $5,000 | 1,282 |
| $ 5,000– 7,499 | 672 |
| 7,500– 9,999 | 374 |
| 10,000–14,999 | 593 |
| 15,000–19,999 | 408 |
| 20,000–24,999 | 313 |
| 25,000–34,999 | 284 |
| 35,000–49,999 | 84 |
| 50,000 or more | 19 |
| Mean household income ... $10,788 | Total number of households 4,029 |

Table 2. Income Distribution of Households of Spanish Origin in Monte Carmelo, 1979

| Income | Number of Households |
|---|---|
| Less than $5,000 | 1,372 |
| $ 5,000– 7,499 | 402 |
| 7,500– 9,999 | 265 |
| 10,000–14,999 | 415 |
| 15,000–19,999 | 202 |
| 20,000–24,999 | 180 |
| 25,000–34,999 | 64 |
| 35,000–49,999 | 36 |
| 50,000 or more | 16 |
| Mean household income ... $8,640 | Total number of households 2,952 |

Tables 1, 2, and 3 provide household income distribution data for Whites, Blacks, and persons of Spanish Origin. Tables 4, 5, and 6 furnish occupation data for the three categories. The information in the tables has been adapted from the U.S. Bureau of the Census (1980: P–13, P–15, P–21).

How do Whites compare with the Blacks and Puerto Ricans living in Monte Carmelo? In terms of mean household income, White households show 14 percent less annual income than Black households and 29 percent more than Spanish Origin households. Also, in terms of households with incomes of $50,000 or more, there are 52 percent less White households in this category than Black households. There are just three less Spanish Origin households

Table 3. Income Distribution of Black Households in Monte Carmelo, 1979

| Income | Number of Households |
|---|---|
| Less than $5,000 | 788 |
| $ 5,000– 7,499 | 252 |
| 7,500– 9,999 | 219 |
| 10,000–14,999 | 351 |
| 15,000–19,999 | 239 |
| 20,000–24,999 | 219 |
| 25,000–34,999 | 122 |
| 35,000–49,999 | 40 |
| 50,000 or more | 29 |

Mean household income ... $12,337

Total number of households 2,259

Table 4. Type of Occupation of White Persons in Monte Carmelo, 1979

| Type of Occupation | Number |
|---|---|
| Managerial and professional | 215 |
| Technical, sales, and administrative support occupations | 1,002 |
| Service occupations | 728 |
| Precision production, craft, and repair occupations | 400 |
| Operatives and laborers | 635 |
| Farming, forestry, and fishing occupations | 24 |
| Total number of employed persons | 3,004 |

Table 5. Type of Occupation of Spanish Origin Persons in Monte Carmelo, 1979

| Type of Occupation | Number |
|---|---|
| Managerial and professional | 200 |
| Technical, sales, and administrative support occupations | 573 |
| Service occupations | 400 |
| Precision production, craft, and repair occupations | 150 |
| Operatives and laborers | 710 |
| Farming, forestry, and fishing occupations | 7 |
| Total number of employed persons | 2,040 |

Table 6. Type of Occupation of Black Persons in Monte Carmelo, 1979

| Type of Occupation | Number |
|---|---|
| Managerial and professional | 213 |
| Technical, sales, and administrative support occupations | 784 |
| Service occupations | 419 |
| Precision production, craft, and repair occupations | 137 |
| Operatives and laborers | 315 |
| Total number of employed persons | 1,868 |

with incomes of $50,000 or more as compared with White households.

In terms of types of occupation, 7 percent of White persons occupy managerial and professional positions compared with 9 percent of the individuals of Spanish Origin and 11.4 percent of the Black workers. The highest percentages of the White and Black work force occupy positions in the technical, sales, and administrative support areas, whereas 35 percent of persons of Spanish Origin are employed as operatives and laborers; 21 percent of the White and 17 percent of the Black workers earn their wages as laborers and operatives.

Household size for the three broad categories of White, Black, and Spanish Origin are 2.66, 3.1, and 3.0, respectively.

While gross socio-econimic data on broad ethnic-racial categories provides one with a general view of what Monte Carmelo has become like in recent years, i.e., a multi-ethnic area, and, as was indicated earlier, an Italian-American enclave has evolved, there are certain caveats that must be recognized.

In presenting comparative ethnic data based on census groupings, one has to be cognizant of the flaws in the classification system. Categories such as "Black," "White," and "Spanish Origin" are not only too broad but confusing as well. The category "Spanish Origin" would include persons from Central and South America, the Spanish West Indies, and Spain. A Mexican Indian immigrant with a knowledge of Spanish would find it difficult to identify himself or herself as a Spanish Origin person. However, in Monte Carmelo most of the Spanish Origin persons are Puerto Ricans.

The "Black" category is equally perplexing. How does one distinguish Black Americans from West Indian Blacks, or

Panamanian Blacks from African Blacks? To be more specific, how does one differentiate Haitian-Americans from Jamaican-Americans, or Ibo Nigerian-Americans from Hausa Nigerian-Americans? My impression is that in Monte Carmelo the Black Americans comprise the largest grouping of the Black population. Similar problems abound with the category "White." In Monte Carmelo, for example, 72 percent of the White population are Italian-Americans. The remaining 28 percent consist of Albanians, Yugoslavians, Irish, Polish, English, German, French, Greek, Hungarian, Portuguese, and a number of others. Despite the fact that virtually all the people I have spoken to stated that there are significant numbers of Albanians and Yugoslavians living in Monte Carmelo, they are not listed in the census tracts under "Ancestry of Persons." It seems to me that these two ethnic groups comprise the majority of the 1,852 people of the White category who did not report their ancestry. It is also likely that a number of Italian-Americans did not report their ancestry. Finally, 528 individuals are listed under multiple ancestry groups of which one of the groups is Italian.

Notwithstanding the deficiencies inherent in the classification of ethnic population by the U.S. Bureau of the Census, the data culled from the census tracts which make up Monte Carmelo provide useful information on the population segments of a multi-ethnic neighborhood.[5] In the next chapter I will examine some of the structural and symbolic aspects of the Italian-American enclave.

## NOTES

1. This whole process may be viewed as networking on an informal and personal basis, the method most preferable to Italian-Americans. Regarding *comare* and *compare* relationships, one must distinguish between the ritual form and the friendship type. In terms of the latter form, when a man refers to another man as *compare*, it very often means friendship of some sort whether it be long term or short-lived. When a man refers to a woman as *compare*, it generally means a mistress. Similarly, a woman's lover would be referred to as *compare*.

2. The family of orientation versus the family of procreaton.

3. Bingo is played two nights a week (Wednesdays and Saturdays) in the basement of the Church of Our Lady of Mount Carmel.

4. The ethnic-racial categories utilized by the U.S. Bureau of the Census in their classification of the population are broad groupings which combine a variety of criteria including national origin, language, pigmentation, and minority status.

5. Household income of Italian-American families described in this chapter is more reflective of the upper ranges of income distribution for Whites as a whole.

According to my information, the average household income of Italian-Americans in general is higher than that of other Whites living in the neighborhood.

# CHAPTER 5

# Structures and Symbols of Community Life

The structural and symbolic expressions of Italian-American ethnicity are manifested in the various community organizations and in the religious rituals and secular festivals which occur throughout the year. This chapter describes the roles of a number of these organizations, including the church, and examines some of the festivals as well.

## THE MERCHANTS ASSOCIATION

One of the most influential organizations is the Market Street and Main Street Merchants Association. Founded in 1973, it has become a powerful force in Monte Carmelo: 126 of the 184 commercial proprietors in Monte Carmelo are members of the Association. Table 7 lists the type and number of business establishments that comprise the Association.

Ninety percent of the 126 businesses are located on Main Street and Market Street. The remaining are situated primarily in residential sections of the community. Eighty percent of the Association's members are Italian-Americans. About 100 merchants commute to their businesses, though most of them had at one time lived in Monte Carmelo.

Members of the Association meet every Tuesday at 7:00 P.M. Often, representatives of other community organizations attend these meetings and, in some instances, serve on the board of directors. At one of the meetings, for example, the head of the Local Development Corporation informed the membership that funds were being made available for small business renovation projects. This type of information is disseminated quickly and efficiently to members of the organization at the weekly meetings. The nearly 60 non-members, on the other hand, are less likely to be readily aware that funds of this sort are obtainable. This would eliminate approximately one-third of the eligible applicants and make more money available for those merchants who apply.

Table 7. Merchants Association Membership

| Type | Number |
| --- | --- |
| Bread Bakery | 4 |
| Cake and Pastry Shop | 4 |
| Restaurant | 6 |
| Luncheonette, Cafe, Pizzeria | 9 |
| Dairy and Cheese | 3 |
| Delicatessen | 5 |
| Pasta Shop | 1 |
| Fish Market | 2 |
| Meat and Poultry | 14 |
| Grocery | 10 |
| Fruits and Vegetables | 11 |
| Wines and Liquors | 2 |
| Automobiles | 2 |
| Bank | 2 |
| Beauty Shop | 3 |
| Clothing | 4 |
| Cleaning | 3 |
| Florist | 1 |
| Gift Shop | 2 |
| Home Furnishings | 4 |
| Merchandise (Sundries) | 6 |
| Jewelry | 4 |
| Records | 2 |
| Travel | 4 |
| Funeral Home | 2 |
| Realty | 2 |
| Construction | 2 |
| Other | 12 |
| Total | 126 |

Adapted from Merchants Association, n.d., *Guide to Monte Carmelo*.

The leadership of the Merchants Association consists of four officers: a president, vice-president, secretary-treasurer, and secretary. In addition, there is a twelve-member board of directors which is headed by a chairman. Proprietors of a supermarket, a hardware store, and a funeral home were some of the past presidents.

Membership fees are $150 a year, part of which is used to defray the cost of the street decorations set up during the Christmas season and every June and July to celebrate the feasts of Saint Anthony and Our Lady of Mount Carmel. From time to time, delinquent members are urged to pay their annual dues so that the Association can more efficiently pursue its goals. Besides the annual fees, merchants may be called upon for special donations to support particular events sponsored by the organization. At one of the meetings the president noted that 41 merchants had made no contributions to promote the "Sale Day" event. Yet these same merchants, according to the president, willingly paid $350 to the New York Chamber of Commerce to have their names appear in its journal. He considered their failure to contribute as a lack of community pride and as a manifestation of poor business sense. Sale Day began as an advertising gimmick in April 1978. Through the years it has developed into a major community event, featuring prizes, gift certificates, and entertainment. Calling it "Family Reunion Week" somewhat tempered the flamboyant quality of the event and had a certain appeal to those from the outside who view Monte Carmelo as the place where kith and kin used to be and, in many instances, still are. The appellation has a homey ring to it, one which rekindles fond memories refracted by the prism of time. It conjures up the sights and sounds and smells of the homes and the streets, the cafés and the stores and, above all, the people. Rather than being merely a commercial event, Family Reunion Week has evolved into an ethnic festival. The decorative display, the busy cafés, and the flow of people along Main and Market Streets, convey the impression that one is participating in an Italian-American event.

Another publicity strategy employed by the Merchants Association to attract business was the Italian Christmas Exhibit at the New York Botanical Gardens. Viewers learned about Italian holiday traditions and about the Monte Carmelo businesses which could help make the holiday season more enjoyable. Visitors picked up guides to the area and received recipe booklets for the special Italian Christmas dishes.

A message that is frequently touted by the Association in its publications or by word of month, especially when members talk to newspaper reporters and magazine writers, is that Monte Carmelo is a safe neighborhood to be in. Over the past five or six years it has received a considerable amount of press coverage, proclaiming it as one of the most secure neighborhoods in the United States. For the Association, this positive image is crucial for their membership's businesses. Conspicuous on the front page of the *Guide to Monte Carmelo*, published by the Merchants Association, are excerpts from articles that appeared in the *New York Times* and *New York* magazine stating that Monte Carmelo is the city's safest neighborhood.

Besides its aggressive efforts to attract shoppers to Monte Carmelo, the Association has played a major role in upgrading the commercial ambience of the community. One of its principal projects
was lobbying for the renovation of the indoor merchants' complex
situated on Market Street. The complex houses small fruit and
produce stands whose owners' margin of profit is slender at best, to
somewhat larger and more profitable housewares, meat, and deli
businesses. The reconstruction was completed at a cost of $600,000
and on April 16, 1983, some forty years after it had been originally
opened by Mayor Fiorello LaGuardia, it was officially reopened
with a grandeur surpassing that of its inaugural celebration. Among
the politicos present were Lieutenant Governor Alfred DelBello,
Mayor Edward Koch, Attorney General Robert Abrams, and
Bronx President Stanley Simon. The presence of Julio DiLorenza,
the Italian Counsel General, was a reminder to both the Monte
Carmelesi and the politicians that the links between Italy and Monte
Carmelo remain strong.

The influence of the Merchants Association extends beyond the
bounds of the commercial world. For some time now the organization has channeled a considerable amount of energy into maintaining the neighborhood as Italian-American turf. This has been
evident in its persistent support for the construction of new apartment complexes; the renovation of old, abandoned dwellings; and
the building of single family private homes, mainly for Italian-
American renters or buyers.

Less than a decade ago, three large apartment high-rises were
constructed on Eastern Boulevard. One was rented out to senior
citizens of whom the largest percentage consisted of Italian-
Americans. Many of the apartments in the two remaining buildings
were also rented out to Italian-Americans and to students attending
a nearby university. The Merchants Association, like other community organizations, attempted to publicize this information so
that it would reach Italian-Americans, or, at least White audiences.
The goal was to bring in Italian-Americans from outside the community. Most of the apartments, however, were rented to Monte
Carmelesi instead. Apparently, many Italian-Americans within the
community were clamoring for better housing and quickly seized the
opportunity to move into new apartments.

More recently the Merchants Association, along with a number of
community organizations, cooperated in an urban renewal program
which resulted in the extensive renovation of three old buildings
located in the vicinity of the church. Most of the funding was

provided by private investors. Efforts were made this time to reach Italian-Americans outside the neighborhood before applications were distributed to Monte Carmelesi. According to my sources, the Council of Monte Carmelo Organizations (COMCO) distributed the applications, and members of the Merchants Association carefully screened the applicants. The church also played a role in the renting process: announcements were made from the pulpit that apartments were available.

Another ambitious enterprise to both attract Italian-Americans from outside to move in, and to keep those in from moving out, has been the construction of fifty one-family homes in the neighborhood. The Merchants Association has been an avid supporter of the project. Once again, the selection process were carefully controlled to insure that virtually all the home buyers would be Italian-Americans.

A qualified buyer would be required to make a down payment of $3,500 and then assume a thirty-year mortgage at a low 6.5 percent interest rate which is guaranteed by the federal government. The homes list for $65,500 but cost the purchaser $51,000, since the government provides a $14,500 subsidy.

Throughout its history, the Merchants Association has played a key role in the maintenance of Italian-American hegemony in Monte Carmelo. Their active involvement in numerous community projects as well as their aggressive publicity program to promote Monte Carmelo as a place to visit, to shop, and to live has been markedly conspicuous in more recent years. The decade of the seventies witnessed the largest outpouring of Italian-Americans from Monte Carmelo in its ninety-year history. Undoubtedly, the founding of the Association in the early seventies was a response to a rising tide of Italian-Americans leaving the community. Within the past few years, according to some observers, there has been a slowing down of the flow. If so, the activities and stratagems of the Merchant Association would have to be considered in the stabilization of the community and in the persistence of Italian-American hegemony.

## COUNCIL OF MONTE CARMELO ORGANIZATIONS

Another association which has played an influential role in the community is the Council of Monte Carmelo Organizations (COMCO). According to a community leader who had been intimately

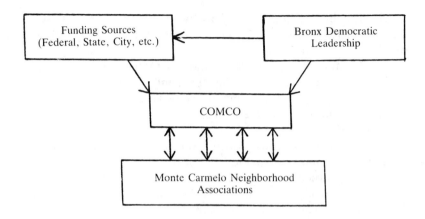

Figure 2. Structural ties of the Council of Monte Carmelo Organizations (COMCO)

associated with it, COMCO functions as an "umbrella-like" type of structure for various community organizations. Because of its many social and economic programs and its accessibility to funding sources and political networks, it supplies information to local groups and, in general, operates as a broker agency for numerous community associations. Figure 2 illustrates the relationships between COMCO and community-based organizations, and between COMCO and sources of funds and influence which lie outside Monte Carmelo. The intent of the diagram is not to convey the impression that relationships occur only in the manner shown. Obviously that would be a misrepresentation, since arrows could be drawn to indicate a direct relationship between a neighborhood association and the Bronx Democratic leadership, or even between a neighborhood association and funding sources. My intention is to demonstrate the significant role COMCO plays in Monte Carmelo by indicating its linkages with community associations and outside sources of power. Its broker position makes it one of the major community organizations. Let us examine the process in a more specific sense.

The Bronx Overall Development Corporation, chaired by the Bronx Democratic Leader, coordinates the programs and the financing of fourteen local development corporations in the Bronx. This involves millions of dollars of federal, state, and city loans and grants to businesses. The allocation of some of these funds for the renovation of a number of stores in Monte Carmelo has been expedited through the political influence wielded by the director of COMCO. By and large COMCO is a Democratic-sponsored and Democratic-functioning community association. Situated next to the local Democratic Club, it has been conspicuous in its support of those candidates for political office who are backed by the Bronx Democratic Leader and by a powerful congressman. A few years ago when Edward Koch and Mario Cuomo were competing in a gubernatorial primary election campaign, the local Democratic politicos were actively campaigning for Koch. Actually, they were simply following orders. The district captain and the director of COMCO were the key party personnel in the local campaign effort. Much to their chagrin, Cuomo handily beat Koch in the Monte Carmelo election district.

Still, the director of COMCO continues to be a powerful figure in the community. As one of the party leaders in Monte Carmelo, he has access to the county leadership and to those programs, job opportunities, grants, loans, and information that the Bronx Democratic leadership dispenses. The political patronage process continues within the community as well. The rewards for loyalty and support are jobs in local community agencies, assistance in obtaining funds for the renovation of one's store or for a community improvement project.

Along with its important broker role, COMCO provides a variety of services for the people of Monte Carmelo such as those related to Medicare, Medicaid, and welfare problems. Some individuals may request assistance in filling out applications for disability claims or social security benefits; qualified tenants and home owners may seek help in applying for a rebate on heat and energy bills; and people exploring career or educational opportunities may utilize the COMCO services. Basically, then, the services furnished by COMCO for the Monte Carmelesi are informational, counseling, and referral.

The structure of COMCO consists of a director who operates as the chairperson of a board of directors. The group holds monthly meetings to consider budget issues, policy, and current projects. The director and members of the board often participate in meetings held by various community associations. The COMCO counselors submit weekly reports to the director and consult with him on a regular basis.

At one time the training and counseling services comprised a significant part of COMCO's efforts. The principal goal of the programs was to teach individuals office skills. As trainees, they were paid $120 a week. In recent years, however, the training program has become virtually moribund as the weekly stipend dropped to $30.

Despite a decline in the community services rendered by COMCO, it continues to be a very influential organization in the community. And, like the Merchants Association, it is committed to preserving Italian-American hegemony in Monte Carmelo. It has supported the construction of apartment complexes and private houses, the renovation of abandoned buildings, the restoration of the Market Street Park, the construction of the Monte Carmelo Branch Library and the Monte Carmelo Cultural Center, to name some of the more conspicuous neighborhood preservation and improvement projects. These efforts, in some instances, were made in cooperation with other associations which together formed the coalition, SON, the acronym for Save Our Neighborhood. The coalition consisted of COMCO, the Merchants Association, Our Lady of Mount Carmel Church, the Monte Carmelo Community Center, and the Neighborhood Development Agency.

For more than twenty years community organizations such as the Merchants Association and the Council of Monte Carmelo Organizations have devoted their efforts to maintaining the Italian hegemony of Monte Carmelo. During the past ten years they have been extraordinarily energetic in their endeavors to stem the outflow of Italian-Americans from the neighborhood. This is especially evident in the area of housing where both associations have played key roles in determining who rents apartments in the newly renovated buildings and who is on the list as potential buyers for the recently constructed private houses. Interestingly, the director of COMCO and most members of the Merchants Association are individuals who commute to Monte Carmelo to work. They are the people who have a high stake in keeping the economic and political power in the hands of Italian-Americans. With some exceptions, these are American-oriented Italian-Americans.


## CLUBS

Among Italian-American males, forms of associational life that have been especially common in neighborhoods like Monte Carmelo are the hometown club and the social club.

Hometown associations have been an integral part of the immigration experience of many ethnic groups who settled in the United States. The Italian immigrant, for example, sought out relatives, friends, and townspeople to live near and with whom they established close bonds. The men often formalized their common bonds by organizing a club. Membership was restricted by gender and birth. In the early years of Italian settlement in communities like Monte Carmelo, these hometown associations were founded by first-generation males, those born in Italy. Their sons born in the United States, the second generation, were also eligible for membership. In addition, membership was open to male offspring of women born in the town but who married men from other towns. In such instances the male offspring would be eligible for membership in more than one association.

Hometown associations flourished in the early years of Italian immigration and continued to attract some members despite a sharp curtailment in Italian immigration in the post-World War I era. On the whole, however, membership declined as fewer second-generation males replaced those of the first generation who died. During the fifties, sixties, and early seventies, a sizeable number of Italians immigrated to the United States. Old hometown associations were emboldened by the new infusion of immigrants and some new organizations were founded. Still, the new immigration could not stay the inexorable atrophy that afflicted most of these organizations.

During the first half of this century, hometown associations were commonplace in the many Italian-American neighborhoods of New York City, including Monte Carmelo. These were organizations with constitutions, officers, elections, and dues. Membership dues were used to pay unemployment benefits for those members who lost their jobs and to help defray the funeral expenses of deceased members.

The early immigrants faced hard times. The few good jobs were difficult to come by, and often those jobs that were available were temporary. Accidents cut short the lives of many men. One such accident killed the father of Pietro Di Donato, the Italian-American author of *Christ in Concrete* (1937). In his novel Di Donato provides us with a poignant account of how Italian-Americans were cowered and brutalized by the social and economic conditions in American society during the twenties and thirties. The author's description of Geremio's death, which was very similar to that of his own father, is undoubtedly the most powerful passage in the novel. Geremio was a foreman on a construction project whose owners kept costs down through shoddy practices. A poorly shored-up building collapsed, and Geremio was thrown against a foundation wall pilaster. Right above him a large concrete hopper broke loose, pouring concrete over his body. The concrete hardened, entombing him. Di Donato graphically describes Geremio's desperate effort to break through the crushing cement. The manner of Geremio's death, like that of the author's father, is a tragic symbol of the entombment of these immigrants and their families in a life of wretchedness. The uncertainty of work and the suddenness of death were part of the reality of the immigrant's life.

Hometown associations furnished material and moral support in times of adversity. In addition, the relatives, friends, and *paesani* who comprised one's association *fratelli* (brothers) provided one with an effective network for seeking out job opportunities or for dealing with the bureaucratic complexities encountered in social and governmental agencies. Furthermore, the hometown association meeting place served as a recreational center for its members. One could play cards, a few games of pool, or just simply enjoy a pleasant conversation while sipping a cup of espresso or bolting down a shot glass of whiskey. Throughout the years, card games have been the single most important recreational activity for many of the members of hometown clubs. At the very least, club rooms were open a few days a week, more often in some instances. Many men spent a substantial part of their leisure time hanging out at the club. From time to time the associations sponsored family recreational activities and dinners which brought together the wives, the children, other relatives, and friends of the members.

The decline in the number of hometown associations in Italian-American neighborhoods reflects demographic and generational changes. In Monte Carmelo, for example, today's Italian-American population is barely 27 percent of what it had been thirty-five years ago. Moreover, a significant number of those who left the community were the young adult males who would normally provide the continuity needed for a viable hometown association.

The young men who continued living in the community could not identify as readily with the more traditional ways of their fathers and consequently few became members of these associations. One such organization in Monte Carmelo faced with dwindling numbers desperately tired to recruit young members. The number of older men remaining in the organization was insufficient to raise the money to pay the rent and maintenance cost required for the club room. Only a few young men responded to their pleas, too few to keep the association functioning. The club ceased to exist. I know of only two hometown associations that continue to operate in Monte Carmelo today. The membership consists of men whose life style could be categorized as Italian oriented.

In Monte Carmelo, social clubs have become the more common form of association. It may be that some of the clubs evolved from hometown associations. Such a situation could develop if a hometown organization broadens its membership by waiving the birth requirement. Friends with ties to different hometowns may be invited to join. A number of these people may be second- and third-generation Italian-Americans. Soon the organization — part hometown association and part social club — begins to evidence a more pronounced intra-ethnic variation, a variation reflective of a changing Italian-American population. Subsequently, as the older first generation die, leadership positions fall to second-generation Italian-Americans. The scenario does not necessarily follow the sequence noted. There could be, of course, situations where recent immigrants are immediately brought into the association and in the process continue to reenforce the Italian quality of the club. However, the development of hometown associations into social clubs would have been more likely to have occurred between 1920 and 1950. At this time considerably fewer Italians emigrated to the United States, yet intra-city migration continued as Italian-Americans moved into and out of Monte Carmelo. During this time a core of second- and third-generation Italian-Americans emerged in the community and played a pivotal role in shaping the cultural content and the social structure of the community.

If some social clubs evolved out of hometown associations, others, perhaps most, were founded by groups of men — joined by bonds of friendship and kinship — who simply wanted a place to hang out, to play cards, to have a few drinks, and to talk about women, cars, and sports. Usually the founders and subsequent members were the more American-oriented Italian-Americans. For people unfamiliar with Monte Carmelo or with Italian-American neighborhoods in general, the club scene conveys an image that frequently reenforces their own distorted views of what Italian-Americans are like. The message communicated by closed doors and opaque windows is clearly that outsiders and non-members are to stay out. Some of the clubs have "For Members Only" signs conspicuously posted on the entrance doors. Suspicions soar. Often outsiders suspect that sinister plots are being concocted behind the locked doors and the darkened windows. The cabalistic ambience, they suppose, is a tell-tale sign of criminal intent.

Outsiders imagine that unlawful activities are the reasons for the secrecy. A more accurate assessment of the happenings in the social clubs would suggest that privacy rather than secrecy is uppermost in the minds of the membership. The emphasis on privacy may have grown out of past experiences with the police. Card playing for money in a club setting was considered gambling. For Italian-Americans, playing cards for money was a social drama and not a criminal act. In the past, clubs were raided and the money confiscated, which often meant bulging pockets for the local precinct police. Clubs were favorite targets and the persistent harassment led to a variety of responses. Spotters were planted to warn the players of an impending police raid. The pay-off, another strategy, often kept the cops away.

A persistent fear of outside threats continues to linger; suspicions endure. The Italian-Americans in their clubs prefer the privacy of each others company. They can exchange barbs and enjoy the companionship of those who have shared similar experiences. The card tables are the focal points for many of the members; others watch television or play pool. Surrounded by the masonry and wood walls which protect them from the prying glances of outsiders, they come to think of their club as a sanctuary, a brief escape from the demands of work and family.

A group of older men form the Monte Carmelo Social Club. This club scene is radically different from that of the more typical social clubs. On most warm evenings the men sit outside to chat and to watch television. They greet friends who pass by, some of whom may stop for a few minutes to converse. Many of the members of the Monte Carmelo Social Club are men who grew up in the neighborhood but have moved out. Some continue to have important business interests in the community. Interestingly, the Democratic Club, COMCO, and the Monte Carmelo Social Club are located just a few yards from one another, and the three of them are controlled by American-oriented Italian-Americans who live outside of the community. In effect, the proximity of these associations on Market Street symbolizes, in spatial terms, the linkages between economic and political interest groups as they are played out in the influential associations of Monte Carmelo.

## CARETAKERS AND LAWBREAKERS

An article in *Il Progresso* (1982: 3) calls Monte Carmelo a "breath of safety" in a dangerous section of the Bronx. Other newspapers and magazines also have described for their readers the relative safety of the neighborhood. For the past six years, especially, this message has been persistently delivered through the media. One type of message reads that one can walk the streets of Monte Carmelo without fear or apprehension. Another kind of message, one that has haunted Italian-Americans for nearly a century, conveys a very different meaning: walk down the streets of Monte Carmelo and you may unwittingly brush by a *mafioso*. One of my colleagues, a professor of anthropology, characterized Monte Carmelo as "mafia territory." This seems to be a logical extension of the "mafia" mentality. Since Italians and Italian-Americans give birth to and nurture *nafiosi*, it would follow that the Italian-American neighborhoods would be swarming with them. The paradox is that a relatively crime-free neighborhood is believed to be inhabited by an inordinate number of notorious criminals.

All neighborhoods have their lawbreakers in one form or another; Monte Carmelo is no exception. There have been killings, burglaries, assaults, and extortion attempts. Gambling has been, and continues to be, the most pervasive of illegitimate enterprises in Monte Carmelo.

Basically, an interpretation of crime and what constitutes criminal activity often varies with the particular ethnic population. For many, Italian-Americans and others, betting on boxing matches, football games, baseball games, horses, and on numbers through an organized gambling network is not viewed as criminal behavior, nor are the street personnel who collect bets thought to be criminals. According to the police — or as one might prefer to call them, the caretakers — the bookies and their bosses are breaking the law. Technically speaking, they are, although many Monte Carmelesi think otherwise.

At this point it is useful to draw a distinction between private gambling and public gambling. Private gambling includes card games played at home, in cafés, in hometown meeting rooms, and in social clubs. Virtually all card games involve betting, and the amounts of money vary. Often players sort themselves out on the basis of low, modest, or high stakes card games. There are players and observers, the latter often sitting in for a hand while the player goes to the bathroom or picks up a drink. Frequently, card playing continues for hours. These games are private social events where friends and kinsmen join together in a major recreational activity, hoping that skill and good luck will combine to bring in a large pot. The drama of the game is clealy visible as players joke, grimace, curse, and, argue.

Some card games are "serious" gambling events in that the stakes are so high that few Monte Carmelesi have the resources to partici-pate. These games may be "sponsored" by specific clubs which receive a share of the winnings. A number of these "gambling houses," according to some of the people that I have spoken to, have slot machines, or as they are sometimes called, "one arm bandits."

The more public form of gambling encompasses a network of collectors or bookies who, in turn, have a network of clients. Usual-ly the bookies have their favorite hangouts where clients can easily find them. They establish personal ties with their steady customers, some of whom may call in a number with the bookie covering the bet. It is important for bookies to have the sort of hangout sites where they have access to phones. People in the community often refer to this type of establishment, whether it be a club or a coffee shop, as a "numbers place" or a "front." Some of my informants told me that one such place is a luncheonette which appears to operate rather successfully as an eatery. On a number of occasions when I ate there, I observed a fairly diverse class of diners. A middle-aged grouping of American-oriented Italian-American males comprised the luncheonette's regulars. They would occupy one or two tables during the "off hours," drink American coffee and eat a muffin or a Danish. The conversations centered on sports. From time to time, the bookie would sit down and talk for a few minutes before resuming his usual position in front of the luncheonette.

A bookie's occupation is not a very enviable one, though some say they can earn "a few hundred dollars a week, clean." One twenty-two-year old man described a bookie as "an uneducated guy who couldn't make it any other way." The bookie is the silent street hawker who sells bets. He is at the lowest echelon of the gambling enterprise. When things heat up at precinct headquarters because of outside pressures from the "brass," the bookies are the people who ae picked up. Usually, the "big guy" posts the bail and provides the necessary legal services for his street and storefront workers. Nor-malcy generally means that the gambling establishment can function practically free of caretaker interference. A *modus operandi* exists between the police and the gambling enterprise mogul(s) — the caretaker–lawbreaker relationship in the area of public gambling has been nurtured by years of accommodation. Recently the New York City Police Department carried out a series of raids on gambling "fronts" in various neighborhoods of Brooklyn, Queens, Manhattan, and the Bronx. Not one "front" in Monte Carmelo was on the list. Perhaps it was because the caretakers were concentrating on the Cuban-American "fronts." Or it may be that the caretakers seek out the less influential gambling organizations to put out of business, temporarily at least. At the same time, the publicity of the mass arrests conveys the message that the police are cracking down on the lawbreakers. Some lawbreakers, however, are less likely to be harassed by the caretakers. The gambling establishment in Monte Carmelo has continued to operate relatively free of police intervention.

The gambling activities in Monte Carmelo are orchestrated by one or more "big guys." A number of individuals in the neighborhood have singled out one particular person, Mr. B., as the most powerful racketeer in the community. He doesn't live in Monte Carmelo but frequently hangs out to take care of business. He reminds one of T.S., the head of gambling activities in Cornerville, an Italian-American community in Boston, described by Whyte (1966) in one of the classics of sociological literature, *Street Corner Society*. Whyte (ibid: 115) describes T.S. as an individual who "works quietly in the background." He had built an efficient organization which continues to operate with a minimum amount of violence. Racketeering, whether it be in Cornerville or in Monte Carmelo, is a business and a T.S. or a Mr. B. function as the corporate heads. In Monte Carmelo someone like Mr. B. has the financial resources to influence both the caretakers and the politicians in order to protect his investments. In addition, he can buy the "muscle" to enforce discipline within the ranks and, in general, to engender an aura of fear which serves as a protective wall against those who we would be foolish enough to violate the code of silence.

There are those people who speak of Mr. B. with reverence and a tinge of trepidation. Some call him the "wise guy"; others refer to him as the "mafia guy." Nobody identifies him by name. The impression one gets is that his power is awesome. One thing is certain — he has considerable influence in Monte Carmelo. Like the

Merchants Association, COMCO, the church, and other community associations, Mr. B. and his gambling organization are concerned with the maintenance of Italian-American hegemony in the neighborhood. Mr. B. supports the various community preservation programs and it is very probable that some of the funds for the renovation of a number of buildings were provided by him. Mr. B's services extend beyond financial assistance; his contacts and advice are also considered important. He is viewed as someone who can do something for you. Certain people believe that his influence could be helpful in resolving problems and, consequently, utilize those links in a fairly expansive network that would open up channels of communication with him. Mr. B. has won a great deal of respect and good will because of his efforts to help the Monte Carmelesi.

Mr. B. operates his gambling business with impunity. His interests and those of the caretakers are very similar. The caretakers choose to deal with a population in which few lawbreaking problems become conspicuous enough to require police action. The caretakers in their patrol cars and on foot prefer the normal routine of community life. Uncontrolled lawbreaking disrupts the natural order and creates uncertainty, confusion, distrust, and fear. To minimize these conditions, methods of resolving potential or actual lawbreaking problems have developed.

An incident took place a few years ago which illustrates one of the ways of dealing with a potentially volatile situation. As mentioned before, the Italian soccer team had won the World Cup and the Monte Carmelesi poured into Main Street to celebrate. Cars decorated with Italian flags moved through the streets of Monte Carmelo, their horns blowing and their occupants cheering wildly. A particularly large crowd formed in Bishop Perone Square. It was one of the most impressive expressions of community solidarity that I had ever seen.

The victory celebration took place late in the afternoon on a Sunday in July. It was also the first Sunday of the week-long feast in honor of Our Lady of Mount Carmel. This meant that four blocks of the main thoroughfare were blocked off and no cars were allowed through thus preventing the car caravans from driving down Monte Carmelo's principal street. As the police put up the barriers, a number of young men attempted to remove them. Soon a large crowd began to press up against the police officers. One policeman in particular became so incensed with the defiance of those who tried to remove the barriers that he rushed into the crowd, determined to take action against a couple of the men. The two other officers assessing the explosive nature of the situation gingerly backed out of the surrounding throng. The one remaining officer was jostled by a couple of the men. No effort was made by the two other officers to assist their partner; no radio call went out for backup policemen. It was as if the two officers recognized that the problem was one that existed between their partner and the community. Somehow it has to be resolved without bringing in additional support units. As the crowd began to press harder around the lone policeman, the pastor of the church moved quickly into the center of the fracas and spoke to the flustered policeman and the angry men. He not only managed to defuse a confrontation type situation, but convinced the men to allow the barriers to stand. The car caravans left Monte Carmelo for other Italian-American neighborhoods. Priests have played important mediator roles between young lawbreakers (or potential lawbreakers), their families, and the police. As the former assistant to the pastor phrased it: "When a youngster gets into trouble, the cops ask us to talk to the family to try to straighten him out. Usually we can do something about it."

From time to time the more prosperous and influential merchants have intervened to resolve lawbreaking behavior. The owner of a café was being victimized by one of the neighborhood punks who would brazenly step up to the cash register and take whatever money he wanted. One customer who frequented the café told me that this had happened a number of times. Rather than report the thefts to the police or try to deal with the thief on a one to one basis, the café owner decided to discuss the problem with one of the wealthiest merchants in Monte Carmelo. The merchant, in turn, had a private conversation with the lawbreaker. The café owner has not been bothered since.

Caretakers also recognize that lawbreakers who enter Monte Carmelo to committ crimes such as burglaries and muggings may in turn become victims of punitive assaults. That is the price that the outsider who preys on the Monte Carmelesi may have to pay. Some of these lawbreakers have been caught by community people, beaten, and then turned over the police. Some have been beaten and turned loose with a stern warning never to enter the neighborhood again.

In many ways the lines that separate the caretakers from the lawbreakers can be quite tenuous, so tenuous in fact, that the caretaker and lawbreaker personnel can exchange roles. Mr. B., the

gambling czar, is an important linkage for both the police and
people in the community when the non-routine lawbreaking activities threaten the normalcy of life. Mr. B. would support all efforts
to apprehend and punish those who hold up shops, clubs, and cafés
in the neighborhood.

   Mr. B. and others like him operate as caretakers in yet another
way. Their interests coincide with those of other community leaders
and interest groups. The merchants, the politicos, the clergy, the
heads of various community social agencies, and even the law en-
forcement caretakers — through their actions, and, in some instances, their policies — are involved in fostering Italian-American
sovereignty in Monte Carmelo. So is Mr. B. Together they are
caretakers of a perduring Italian-American ethnicity.


## OUR LADY OF MOUNT CARMEL

Both as a symbol and as an organization, Our Lady of Mount
Carmel is undoubtedly the most prominent conveyance of *Italianita*
in the community. It stands as an imposing strucuture at the very
hub of business and social activity. As the daily stream of people
move past its doors on Main Street, many of them quickly bless
themselves. Some go in for the weekday 8:00 A.M. mass conducted
in Italian. Others prefer the English evening mass at 7:30. Masses,
novenas, rosary recitations, Lenten services, such special holiday
services as those held on Christmas and Easter, and the life-cycle
services including baptism, first holy communion, confirmation,
marriage, and the funeral mass provide the Monte Carmelesi with
the liturgical continuity and routinization which reflect the natural
flow of life. For eighty years Our Lady of Mount Carmel has
affected the lives of the people in very significant ways.

   When the Italians first settled in Monte Carmelo they attended
mass at St. Philip Neri, a newly constructed church located some
distance from the community.[1] A few years earlier, Father Daniel
Burke had been sent specifically to minister to the Italians who had
quickly become the third largest foreign population in the area. As
the Italian population increased, a number of Monte Carmelesi
pressured the then Monsignior Burke to open a mission in their
community. He agreed and on June 13, 1906, the feast day of St.
Anthony of Padua, a storefront church was opened on Main Street.
Father Joseph Caffuzzi, a young priest from Milan, was placed in

charge of the misson. This small storefront chapel served an esti-
mated 3,000 Catholics and it soon became evident that a larger and
more permanent structure would be needed. Plans were made for
the construction of a basement church and in a little over a year,
July 16, 1907, the feast day of Our Lady of Mount Carmel, mass
was offered in the new building. For the next ten years, services
were held in the basement church while the building of the entire
church continued. In the meantime there was a rapid growth in the
Italian-American population as evidenced by the number of baptisms. There were only 43 performed in the storefront chapel;
however, after the completion of the basement church in 1907, the
number had increased to 115. Baptisms nearly tripled over the next
year. By 1916, the year before the church building had been completed, 1,158 infants were baptized.

In October 1917 the church was officially blessed and thousands
of children paraded in the streets of Monte Carmelo in celebration.
In eleven years and three months the storefront chapel had been
transformed into an imposing Romanesque edifice overlooking the
streets, businesses, and homes of the Monte Carmelesi. Finally, the
people of the community had their church, a monument to their
patience and labourious efforts. The vast majority had only recently
emigrated from their towns in southern Italy where the visual presence of the church and the sound of its bells were part of the
natural order. The church was an integral part of the folk traditions
of the people, a symbolic and physical context for the ritual drama
of the life cycle. The church, regardless of how frequent or how
rarely one entered its doors, and regardless of how one reacted to
its theological precepts and its priests, had a life force of its own to
which the people responded. The Monte Carmelesi wanted to re-
capture the essence of their churches and to share a common religious experience which distinguished them from Irish and German
Catholics living in the general area.

As church membership grew, the religious associations and activities also increased. Some of the early orgaizations were the Angels,
St. Aloysius Sodality, Children of Mary, League of the Sacred
Heart, Catholic Club, Schola Cantorium, Aspirants, Holy Name
Societies (American and Italian), Catholic Boys Brigade, and the
Conference of St. Vincent de Paul. In 1923, the Pallotine Sisters,
under the sponsorship of the church, opened the first daycare center
in the community to provide care for the preschool children of
working mothers, many of whom worked in local seamstress shops.

In 1924 Our Lady of Mount Carmel officially inaugurated a parochial education program with the enrollment of 100 boys and 105
girls. For twenty-five years boys and girls attended classes in an old
building which had, at one time, housed the homeless. On October
17, 1949 the new school building was opened. During the mid-fifties
as many as 1,800 children attended Our Lady of Mount Carmel and
about 95 percent were Italian-Americans. At about the same time
construction was completed on a convent to house the nuns who
taught in the school. Today the number of students in the school is
nearly one-third of what it had been thirty years ago and about
45–50 percent are Italian-Americans.

In reviewing the eighty-year history of Our Lady of Mount Carmel, the years 1930–1960 represent a special era in its development.
Despite the 1936 fire which destroyed a substantial part of the
church, the rebuilding was completed in less than a year and a half
and the church continued to grow and to prosper. Under Father
Perone's tenureship as pastor during the forties and fifties, numerous building projects were undertaken and completed. The parochial school, in particular, was one of his main interests. Though
small and frail looking, Father Perone had boundless energy and a
certain charisma which affected many of those who came in contact
with him. He raised nearly one million dollars to build the school.
And from the pulpit and in personal conversations with parishioners
in the streets he appealed to the parents to send their children to the
school. Many responded as evidenced by the large enrollment during the 1950s. Father Perone's work in the parish received wider
recognition. On May 5, 1954 he was consecrated as Auxiliary
Bishop of New York, the first Italian-American Bishop of the
Archdiocese of New York. In later years, after his official retirement from the priesthood, Bishop Person continued to maintain ties
with Our Lady of Mount Carmel. Every spring he would return to
preside over the confirmation ritual of the youth that were always
very dear to him. When he died in 1985, the Monte Carmelesi of all
ages, and those who left the community in years past, came to the
church to pay homage to someone who was both special and yet one
of their own. The church was packed with people standing in the
aisles two abreast and in the rear extending three rows deep. It was
a moving and profound expression of love and respect for the
community's most prominent religious leader.

During Bishop Perone's pastorate, attendance at Sunday mass
often reached 3,000, and many more were present on Palm Sunday,

Easter, and Christmas. In the mid-fifties, there were ten priests all Italian or Italian-American — celebrating eleven Sunday masses, a number of which were conducted in Latin and Italian. On holy days, ten masses were celebrated and, again, a number of these were Latin-Italian masses. This was also true of the six daily weekday masses.

Today the Italian-American population is less than 30 percent of what it was thirty-five years ago. Figures for mass attendance (Saturday evening and Sunday) range from about 1,300–1,400 with nearly double that number attending on special holidays. Notwithstanding the percipitous drop in the Italian-American population in the sixties and especially the seventies, the number of masses offered in Italian remains fairly high. Saturday evening and Sunday masses number eight, three of which are in Italian. Three of the seven holy day masses are in Italian and so are two of the four weekday masses. All of the other masses are celebrated in English. The Sunday High Mass at eleven o'clock in the morning is an Italian mass. This has been a tradition in Monte Carmelo for decades.

Today there are five priests affiliated with the church. The pastor is an Italian-American with more of an American orientation than any of the previous pastors. One of the two associates is the more Italian oriented of the three full-time resident priests. The second associate, a recent replacement for one of the more popular priests (Father Rispoli) does not have an Italian surname, nor does the recently appointed principal of the parish school.

Father Rispoli, a portly man in his forties, was born and raised in the community. He was assigned as an associate to the pastor of Our Lady of Mount Carmel at a time when the community was undergoing momentous demographic changes. Father Rispoli — like the merchants, the local politicos, Mr. B., and the heads of various community agencies — was very much concerned about the future of Monte Carmelo. And the future of the community was dependent on stemming the flow of Italian-Americans out of the area and preserving Italian-American hegemony. Father Rispoli was known to many of the influential people in the community and, like most of them, he was more American oriented than Italian oriented. Despite his status as associate to the pastor, he subsequently beame the most powerful priest in the parish. His position was further solidified when the pastor suffered a heart attack and he became the *de facto* head of the church. As the administrator he virtually controlled all church activities including the school, the feasts, bingo, and fund raising, to name some. He also worked closely with the police in dealing with young lawbreakers. In addition to all of his church-related responsibilities, Father Rispoli was an active member of a number of community preservation organizations. His role as administrator proved advantageous in enlisting church support for community preservation projects. The pulpit can be an effective communication mode in informing people about housing opportunities in the community.

Interestingly, Father Rispoli's family had moved out of Monte Carmelo approximately twenty years ago. His role had been much like that of other community leaders and businessmen who had left the community for other parts of the Bronx and the suburbs but return to conduct business, to head a social agency, or to administer a school. Father Rispoli returned and stayed on to assume an important leadership role in the church and the community at a time when the community was experiencing major demographic changes. Recently Father Rispoli left Monte Carmelo to serve as pastor of a church in Yonkers.

Throughout the years, Our Lady of Mount Carmel has played a crucial role as a cardinal symbol of *Italianita* and as an active community organization. Recent changes in the church's leadership may signal new directions although, at this point, there has been no evidence of any major policy shifts. Whether the pastor or one of his associates can deal as ably with community leaders as Father Rispoli had remains to be seen.

## FEASTS AND PROCESSIONS

The two principal feast days celebrated in Monte Carmelo are St. Anthony on June 13 and Our Lady of Mount Carmel on July 16. Despite the fact that Our Lady of Mount Carmel is the patron saint of the community, St. Anthony appears to be the more important of the two. This is discernible in the longer time period devoted to the secular celebration and in the protracted procession though the streets of the neighborhood.

Older informants describe the elaborate feasts of the past when decorations could be seen for many blocks and booths were set up all along Main Street from Eastern Boulevard to beyond Market Street. Even some of the side streets had booths and decorative displays. Those were the days when bands played Italian music and the musicians donned white caps and dark suits. Fireworks lit the sky as children, awed and frightened at the same time, nestled up to their mothers whose thoughts were of another time and another place.

In the towns of Calabria, Campania, and other provinces of southern Italy, feast days, often commemorating the towns' patron saints, were very special days when family, friends, and *paesani* joined in a common celebration. Town saints were a special source of pride for the people and feasts were opportunities to compete with neighboring towns. From time to time the competition was manifested in brawls involving young men from rival towns. This happens today in Monte Carmelo when "the Italians from Morris Park or from Allerton Avenue" make themselves conspicuous in the neighborhood. Hispanics and Blacks are also targets. The old town rivalry has been transformed into inter-neighborhood and inter-ethnic altercations.

Older informants describe the feasts in their towns as three-day events compared with those in Monte Carmelo which extend for a period of twelve days. The twelve-day version of the feast is undoubtedly related to its money-producing role. Father Rispoli once described the feasts as important fiscal events. He stated it in this manner: "The money we make pays the parish school teachers' salaries for July and August." The church receives $75 per booth per day. In addition, money is generated from gambling activities which are held in the basement of the church. In the past two years the Feast of Our Lady of Mount Carmel has been cut to five days. There has been some speculation that the merchants with stores on Main Street were complaining that the booths reduce the number of parking spaces and, as a result, prospective customers go elsewhere. The argument apparently did not disuade Father Rispoli and the former pastor from continuing with the twelve-day event. The shorter Our Lady of Mount Carmel feast has been associated with the new pastor. Perhaps the merchants have been more persuasive in their arguments or perhaps the new pator has his own ideas about the format of the feast.

In Italy the procession takes place on the feast day immediately after the mass honoring the particular saint or the Madonna. Not so in Monte Carmelo where the procession is held on the Sunday closest to the feast day. On July 17, 1983, the day after the official feast day, I participated in the procession in honor of Our Lady of Mount Carmel. The description that follows has been excerpted from my field notes.

The preparations for the procession began in front of the church at about 5:30 P.M. A number of men rolled out the platform and readied the stand for the statue which was carried out of the church about ten minutes later. Flowers and scapulas adorned the statue of the Madonna.

Before the procession began, a band played the U.S. national anthem and the Italian national anthem. Leading the procession were two rows of women, members of the Mount Carmel Sodality, followed by the band which, in turn, was followed by the priests and the dignitaries. Behind the priests was the statue of Our Lady of Mount Carmel mounted on a movable stand pushed by a number of men. Following the statue were a large number of females of all ages, some older and middle-aged men, very few young men, and a number of boys. As the procession moved through the streets of the neighborhood, people came forward to buy scapulas and to make donations. A few older women approached the statue, kissed their fingers, and tenderly stroked the arms of the Madonna. Some were crying. A woman and her son, who appeared to have Down's syndrome, were holding the stand bearing the statue. There were others walking alongside the Madonna as they have been doing year after year, each hoping for that special miracle.

For more than two hours the procession traced a path through and around a section of the traditional neighborhood of Monte Carmelo. In a symbolic expression of space, the procession outlined the major streets, the main residential areas, and the boundaries of the Italian-American enclave.

In addition to the two major processions, St. Anthony and Our Lady of Mount Carmel, there are two minor ones. A procession in May in honor of the Madonna of Monte Verde and one in September for Our Lady of Sorrows are the less important street processions in Monte Carmelo in that a much smaller percentage of people participate and the area covered consists of just a few blocks.

The feasts, the street festivals, the processions, and the church itself express, in part, the Italian quality of the community. They are, to a greater or lesser degree, symbols of *Italianita* and, as such, contribute to the cultural image projected by the Monte Carmelesi.

# NOTES

1. Attsubstantial amount of the historical information on Our Lady of Mount Carmel comes from sources such as the *Golden Jubilee of Our Lady of Mount Carmel 1906–1956* (1956) and a number of souvenir journals commemorating special events in the church's history.

CHAPTER 6

# Italian-American Ethnicity: Myths, Metaphors and the Mafia Image

A variety of issues which surround Italian-American ethnicity are considered in this chapter. The issues themselves are explored within the setting of the community of Monte Carmelo itself and, also, within the broader framework of the Italian-American ethnic population.

## MONTE CARMELO: THE LITTLE ITALY OF THE BRONX

One of the most persistent misconceptions has been the view that Monte Carmelo is an Italian neighborhood. To some degree, perhaps, this perception has been reenforced by media focus on the Italian-American segment of the population, a focus which has been especially salutary for the local merchants, clergy, and politicians. In reality, the traditional Monte Carmelo, which had at one time extended much beyond the current boundaries of the enclave, is a multi-ethnic neighborhood. Indeed, boundaries in recent years have become less rigid as the frequency and intensity of violence has tapered off. Demographic figures alone clearly demonstrate the multi-ethnic quality of the neighborhood. As recently as the 1960s, one could discern the beginnings of a population shift which would virtually overwhelm those Italian-Americans still living in the neighborhood during the seventies and early eighties. By 1980, the Italian-American population was a mere 25 percent of what it had been some forty years past and one-third of what it was two decades ago. In twenty years, 1960–1980, the Italian-American population of Monte Carmelo dropped by nearly 14,000. As Italian-Americans left, Puerto Ricans, Blacks, Yugoslavians, Albanians, Koreans, Cubans, and others came to replace them. Puerto Ricans, alone, comprise 41 percent of the population of the traditional Monte Carmelo, which makes them the largest ethnic group in the neighborhood; Italian-Americans are the second largest group, accounting for 33 percent of the population; and Black-Americans, numbering 4,500, are the third largest ethnic group. In addition, there are approximately 1,500–

2,000 Albanians and Yugoslavians in Monte Carmelo. About ten other ethnic groups in the area comprise a relatively small percentage of the population.

The Little Italy of the Bronx is no longer the 100 square blocks where nearly 28,000 Italian-Americans lived and where many of them shopped, played, worshipped, and worked. It has become an enclave in which symbols and structures, people and events, manifest ethnicity and define boundaries.

What is the essence of this enclave which generates a larger-than-life image of Italian ethnicity? Basically Monte Carmelo, the enclave, represents a curious interplay of a specific kind of cultural imagery and a structural nexus of community organizations. Essentially, the cultural imagery is a projection of that aspect of Monte Carmelo which is quintessentially Italian. The Italian language becomes a primary marker of the ethnic character of the enclave. People who speak English or Spanish or Croatian are perceived merely as supernumeraries who have little or no affect on the ethnic quality of Monte Carmelo. Yet the common display of Italian food and Italian wares along Main Street and Market Street are persistent visual cues which trigger off a singular response: "This is the kind of food and goods you can find only in an Italian neighborhood." Pizza parlors, restaurants, cafés, bread stores, and pastry shops are frequently encountered as one strolls through the community. The image of food becomes an ethnic metaphor, a representation of an ethnic collectivity. Similarly, street processions, feasts, and such events as the spontaneous celebration following the winning of the World Cup by Italy further reenforce the image of *Italianita* which is so often associated with Monte Carmelo.

If the imagery is Italian, the structure is primarily Italian-American, with most of the organizations controlled by the American-oriented Italian-Americans. The enclave structure is a texture of linkages, tying together a variety of organizations such as the Merchants Association, COMCO, the church, the Monte Carmelo Neighborhood Association, and others. Also, lawbreakers and caretakers comprise an integral part of the texture. At times the texture is stretched and torn by conflict or factionalism; still, the basic structure seems to hold together. The politicos, most of the merchants, the heads of community agencies, the gambling czar, the caretakers and, in a sense, the priests are outsiders who control the community and exert an influence which spills over the boundaries of the enclave. Most of these outsiders are American-oriented

Italian-Americans who had grown up in Monte Carmelo and subsequently moved out. It is they who benefit most from the perception that Monte Carmelo is an all-Italian community. Still this curious interplay between cultural imagery and structural form sheds some light on the nature of ethnic persistence and ethnic change among those Italian-Americans who live or work in Monte Carmelo. Despite the fact that the community is a remnant of a more extensive Italian-American neighborhood, it has within it a certain vitality and durability which could very well mean many more years of a strong Italian-American presence. Many of the Italian-Americans who have stayed on live in private homes. The value placed on living in one's own home and cultivating a plot of land, however small, has been part of the ethnic legacy. Two-family homes are particularly popular since married offspring can live upstairs. Homes in Monte Carmelo are relatively inexpensive compared with some other neighborhoods in the Bronx or in the suburbs. The emphasis on private ownership has been buttressed recently by the construction of about fifty homes under a federal program to provide subsidized housing for families with limited incomes. As was noted in Chapter 5, virtually all the units were sold to Italian-Americans. Those fortunate enough to buy the houses were selected by the local powerbrokers and members of influential community associations.

The history of Monte Carmelo has been one of change. During its formative years and throughout the golden decades of the thirties, forties, and fifties, people moved in and out. Some stayed on for just a few years and then left to buy homes or to rent apartments in other communities, many of which also had large percentages of Italian-Americans. Others remained for longer periods of time. And there were those who lived out their lives in Monte Carmelo.

The stability of the community was viewed in terms of its persistent Italian-American population, one which was in constant flux as people moved in and out. Moreover, the population itself was not homogeneous, but reflected cultural variations and class differences. The parameters of Italian-American ethnicity ranged from Italian-oriented types to American-oriented types, yet the overall perception was one of an Italian community. In more recent times the demographic changes have dramatically altered the ethnic composition of the neighborhood. Still the perception persists, now perhaps, in more pronounced and publicized forms. Under the guise of *Italianita* there lurks a power base of merchants, politicos, caretakers and lawbreakers, priests, heads of community agencies, and others who reap the benefits of maintaining Italian-American hegemony. Many of these are outsiders, those American-oriented Italian-Americans who are, in reality, true insiders. A community like Monte Carmelo, its people and their cultural styles, its numerous associations, its church, its rituals, and its present status provides us with some insight into the dynamics of ethnicity in general and into Italian-American ethnicity in particular. In reflecting on the demographic changes over the past twenty-five years, one's immediate response would be that Monte Carmelo's identity as an Italian-American community is rapidly fading. There are those who view it as another ethnic ghetto whose time has come and, like many others, it will soon become yet another group's ethnic ghetto.

Given its social-demographic profile, it is difficult to deny that Monte Carmelo is no longer the Italian-American neighborhood it once had been. Nevertheless, its status as an Italian-American enclave contributes to the maintenance of Italian-American ethnicity in areas beyond its borders. Italian-Americans living in other communities of the Bronx, in New Jersey, Westchester County, Long Island, and Connecticut drive to Monte Carmelo to shop; to visit relatives; to eat at restaurants; to participate in club activities; to attend hometown association meetings and community organization meetings; to hear mass in Italian; to celebrate a wedding; to mourn a friend or kinsperson; to hang out; and to enjoy the feasts, street festivals, and cultural events at the Monte Carmelo Cultural Center. Monte Carmelo, the enclave, is a vibrant focal point of Italian-American activities. In its many festive and ritual roles, it is a celebration of Italian-American ethnicity.

The network of kinspeople and friends extends to many neighborhoods and areas of the metropolitan region. It includes those who live a short distance away in various Bronx communities with high percentages of Italian-Americans: Morris Park, Middletown, Country Club, Schuylerville, Throgs Neck, Pelham Parkway, and Baychester. The network links up the Monte Carmelesi with people in Yonkers, Eastchester, Harrison (Westchester County), Rockland County, Queens County, Nassau County, Suffolk County, and Bergen County, to name just a few specific and general areas. Moreover, there are those former Monte Carmelesi who live hundreds of miles, and some even father away, yet they continue to maintain ties with the community. In southern California, for example, there is a Monte Carmelo Association consisting of former residents of the "old neighborhood" who still keep in touch with friends and relatives living in the community. Although Monte Carmelo's populace is multi-ethnic, the community serves as an ethnic mecca for thousands of Italian-Americans. Some Italian-Americans travel to the community on a regular basis. Others visit rarely, if at all, but still perceive themselves as past residents of a pristine ethnic neighborhood whose people and life style have become for them an enduring symbol of Italianism. There are other Italian-American communities in New York; Boston; Philadelphia; New Haven, Connecticut; Providence, Rhode Island; Hoboken, New Jersey; St. Louis; Chicago; San Francisco; New Orleans; and in other cities and towns that have been and, in many cases, continue to serve as ethnic meccas for Italian-Americans. Some, like Monte Carmelo and the North End of Boston, have become enclaves sustaining their role as symbols of ethnicity for large numbers of Italian-Americans both near and far. Like the towns and cities of Calabria, Sicily, Apulia, Campania, and other regions of Italy from which the immigrants came, ethnic neighborhoods provide a spatial identification for the newcomers and their descendants as they adapt to new situations and new environments. The new and the old become integrated into a collective symbol of Italian-American ethnicity. This process reflects the dynamic nature of ethnic phenomena. New space and old space become part of an ever-changing pattern of ethnic symbolism. The symbolic character of the particular space called "Monte Carmelo" transcends the boundaries of the community, linking up with other Italian-Americans in other spaces, and thus serving as a spatial center-piece of Italian-American ethnicity. The community's persistent symbolic role depends, of course, on the viability of its' structural components, i.e., the organizational structure and interacting personnel. Monte Carmelo's durability as the premier Italian-American community of the Bronx seems assured for the remainder of this century at least, if not longer.

## ITALIAN-AMERICAN ETHNICITY AND THE ASSIMILATION ISSUE

One of the major issues plaguing the Italian-American population in recent years is one that revolves around the question of the extent that this group has assimilated into United States society. The question of assimilation has resurfaced in recent years mainly as a response to the flurry of interest in ethnic revivalism or the "New Ethnicity." Moreover, ethnicity and assimilation have become increasingly viewed by some as manifestations of class phenomena. This issue will be discussed in general terms and then will be considered more specifically in the context of the Italian-American experience.

The consensus among the pro-assimilationists is that the process is unidirectional and involves basically two parties: the guest represented by the foreign population, the ethnic group, and the host, or the group that has become the historical model for the receiving society. The convergence between the ethnic population and the present-day representatives of the historical model expresses the extent of assimilation. The assumption is that all groups will, or at least should, approach the model population in terms of socio-cultural characteristics. Ideally all ethnic groups ought to replicate the model, thereby validating the American way.

Essentially, the assimilationist view is predicated on an ideological perspective which perceives our society as a relatively open system and accepts a particular life style — that of the core group or model population — as desirable. In essence, assimilation, in the imagery of its advocates, ultimately leads to the greatest good for the greatest number.

The greatest good for the greatest number, according to the implicit ideology of the assimilationists, can only be attained in a society whose structure facilitates upward mobility through education, occupational and business opportunities, equal access to a wide variety of consumer items, and a relatively open networking system which provides linkages with individuals of different backgrounds, some of whom may become friends, affines, members of the same associations, co-workers, colleagues, etc. It would be a logical extension of the assimilationists' view to incorporate class categories as rungs of a ladder leading upward. Needless to say, ladders are just as readily used to descend as to climb. For the assimilationists, most ethnics climb upward. Those who stay behind are very likely to be victims of racism, long years of economic impoverishment, or ethnic stereotyping and the subsequent consequences. These cracks in the wall are minor flaws; the structure is still sound. The class assimilationists argue that in time ethnic groups are transmuted into class groupings. Most become members of the middle class. The more fortunate ones enter the upper middle class, that rather exclusive category which includes affluent professionals, executives, and successful business entrepreneurs. Curiously, the class assimilationists have very little to say about the upper class. On the other hand, they have a great deal to say about the working class. Notwithstanding the long term use of "working class," the nomenclature still strikes me as rather strange considering that, with few exceptions, all of us work for wages. For the assimilationists, however, the working class category consists of operatives, craftspeople, and others who presumably use their hands more than their intellect. Those who are more ostensibly ethnic, according to the class assimilationists, are people of the working class category; those less so are in the middle stratum; and those least so are presumably in the upper middle class category. It is the American dream played out in the imagery of the class assimilationists. This interplay of class and ethnicity in the assimilation process is manifested in the work of a number of American social scientists who have written about Italian-Americans in particular or ethnicity in general.

One of the most prominent and the one who, perhaps, has had the greatest impact on the thinking of social scientists concerned with the issue of the relationship between ethnicity and class is Herbert Gans. His research on Italian-Americans living in the West End of Boston was published in an influential monograph, *Urban Villagers*, which first appeared in the early 1960s, was subsequently reprinted a number of times, and was recently revised. A substantial amount of the data incorporated in the book was collected during a seven-month residence in a community where the Italian-American population comprised 42 percent of the total (Gans 1982:8).

After several careful readings of the monograph, I became convinced that some of Gans' perceptions of Italian-Americans were based on a limited exposure to the wide range of variation within the Italian-American population living in the West End, as well as misconceptions which may reflect his own expectations of Italian-American social, cultural, and intellectual styles.

For example, in a discussion on how the Italian-American child learns to deal with words and needs, Gans explains in a footnote that "words are used as means to an end, rather than as conceptual tools. This may explain why the Italian-American community has produced so few analytically inclined intellectuals, but a larger number of critical and moralizing polemicists. For they also have come out of working-class parental backgrounds similar to those in the

West End" (ibid.:61). Gans' field of generalization has extended from a short-term observation of some Italian-Americans living in a particular neighborhood of Boston to an entire ethnic population, past and present.

His putative understanding of the cognitive processes of Italian-Americans in general (as noted above) and West End Italian-Americans in particular is further evidenced in his analysis of the failure of the West Enders to respond to education. Gans writes that "educational achievement depends largely on the ability to absorb and manipulate concepts, to handle the reasoning processes embedded in the lesson and the text, and to concentrate on these methods to the exclusion of other concerns. *West End Children are adept at none of them* (emphasis mine)" (ibid.:133). How can one make such a generalization with little or no data to substantiate the statement? Gans interviewed three principals, two of whom were Irish-Americans. He did not interview any of the teachers. More importantly, how well did Gans know the Italian-American students?

In addition to his insights into the uneducable nature of West End Italian-American children, Gans presumes to be equally informed about latent homosexuality among Italian-American males. According to Gans, "many Italian men, *of course* (emphasis mine), do evince the kind of vanity regarding their physical and sexual powers, and the concern with their physysical appearance and dress that is usually identified with latent homosexuality" (ibid.:63).

Italian-Americans who have succeeded in "contemporary popular music," have done so because this form of music "emphasizes the development of an individual image and style more than technical musical skill" (ibid.:83). Apparently, Gans' expertise extends beyond sociology and psychology and includes musicology as well.

The distinction between object-oriented behavior and person-oriented behavior is, for Gans, a crucial conceptualization of the differences between the working class and the middle class. He views the West Ender as having "considerable difficulty in understanding object-oriented behavior," and consequently, "is unable to visualize people organized in cooperative group activity toward a common goal" (ibid.:95). Later he writes that

The person-oriented West Ender, however, does not live in this society [whatever this means]. His social life takes place in peer groups that are not given to cooperative activity or purposive goal-seeking. Indeed, much of his behavior is based on impulsive, but time-tested, reactions to the people he has known since childhood — a type of social life that does not encourage or require the detachment demanded in voluntary organizations. Thus, the West Ender develops a different "me," with a different type of "generalized other," and operates *without a self image* (emphasis mine) (ibid.: 98-99).

This is a rather puzzling generalization for a number of reasons. Social life occurs in different contexts, not merely in a peer group setting. One's family and kindred provide a network of blood, affinal, and ritual ties which often extend beyond the bounds of one's community, whether it be the West End or Monte Carmelo. In addition, the workplace, clubs and community organizations, church activities, and in general those social activities which occur outside of the community setting, often involve individuals in interpersonal relationships which are not necessarily of a peer group nature.

The statement that West Enders operate "without a self image" is perplexing, in view of the fact that Gans as a social scientist ought to recognize that all humans undergo a socialization experience and, in the process, develop an image of themselves which has both social and personal attributes. West Enders in particular and Italian-Americans in general are no less adept in experiencing a "detachment and self-consciousness" about their activities and about themselves.

In his discussion of consumer goods and mass media, Gans writes: "The choice of goods and entertainment is also regulated by a set of esthetic principles that guide West Enders into accepting only what they think beautiful or pleasurable. While these principles are used unconsciously, and terms such as taste, culture, or art are never heard, West Enders still know what they like, and whenever possible, choose accordingly" (ibid.: 182). The statement presumes a uniformity of esthetic principles in the Italian-American population of the West End. Furthermore, it appears that Gans has demonstrated an impulsive predilection for unsubstantiated generalizations and a lack of understanding of the conscious processes involved in esthetic choices.

At one point, Gans notes that West Enders demonstrate a lack of interest in saving and yet prefer paying cash for what they buy. He does indicate, however, that some people finance car purchases while others buy them outright. Gans then makes a rather interesting statement: "As most West Enders do not have such cash reserves, I suspect that those who paid cash for automobiles were using *sub-rosa* income" (ibid.: 186). Evidently, West Enders are very different from the Monte Carmelesi and other Italian-Americans I have known who made great sacrifices to save money to buy homes, cars, to finance a daughter's wedding or a child's college education, to help their children purchase homes, or to return to Italy to live a modestly comfortable life. Nevertheless, what is most disturbing is Gans' supposition that all West Enders are not savers and, therefore, those people paying cash for big items such as cars probably are using "*sub-rosa* income." Clearly, it is difficult in this situation to draw the line between an impressionistic statement and a stereotypical one. The problem is further exacerbated by yet another statement that Gans makes later in his discussion of the media: "Many Italian singers are — or are said to be — aided by racketeers who invest in their careers and pay the costs that accrue on the road to success" (ibid.: 192). Cash reserves and a successful singing career are evidence of either criminal behavior or of being sponsored by those who are engaged in criminal activities. These egregious misrepresentations of the Italian-American population under the guise of a community study does little to enhance our knowledge of this particular ethnic group. Quite the contrary, it reenforces the imagery of criminality which has plagued Italian-Americans for more than a century.

After reading and re-reading *Urban Villagers*, including the most recent edition which, incidentally, no longer displays a picture of a pathetic waif on its cover, I am left with the impression that it is more contrived than genuine. Armed with certain expectations about the social and cultural patterns of the blue-collar workers or the working class and Italian-American ethnics whose social, cultural, and intellectual styles purportedly coalesce with that of the working class, and indeed, serve as the archetypical form, Gans' interpretation of Italian-American life in the West End of Boston is, in my mind, a mixture of fact and fiction. Had he divested himself of some of his preconceived conceptual schema for analyzing data, avoided the propensity to stereotype behavior and immersed himself more fully in the Italian-American community for a longer period of time, then perhaps a more realistic portrayal of the Italian-American West Ender would have emerged.

Approximately twenty years after Gans began his research in the West End of Boston, James Crispino (1980) initiated a research project on the assimilation of Italian-Americans. Crispino focused on Italian-Americans in Bridgeport, Connecticut and its suburbs. Most of his data is based on 469 returns of a mail questionnaire. Crispino's views, like those of Gans, reflect the class assimilationist's perspective. In the Preface to Crispino's book, *The Assimilation of*

*Ethnic Groups: The Italian Case*, Gans anticipates Crispino's conclusions and affirms "that Italian-Americans are continuing to assimilate: giving up cultural practices, membership in Italian formal and informal groups, and ethnocentric attitudes. In short, the straight line theory which proposes a decline in ethnicity with every generation in America, is upheld." (1980: v) Still, blue-collar workers maintain ethnic patterns while white-collar workers become assimilated. The persistence of ethnic patterns, in the thinking of both Gans and Crispino, would be a class related phenomenon. What this suggests, it would seem to me, is that as long as you're a blue-collar worker you're an ethnic. Once you become a white-collar worker you lose your ethnic characteristics and take on class-related traits. Blue-collar workers of whatever generation are members of a particular class — the working class — and consequently maintain ethnic styles, whereas the middle class of the third generation evidence little if any ethnicity, though Gans does stipulate that "symbolic ethnicity" continues in the third generation. Symbolic ethnicity is "an awareness of, and pride in, Italian-American identity" (ibid.: vi). This is the last vestige of ethnicity among third-generation middle class Italian-Americans.

Crispino echoes Gan's views when he states that "class standing is crucial in determining the role of ethnicity in the lives of Italian-Americans" (ibid.: 146). For the working class, it is manifested on the behavioral level. These are the people who "live" their ethnicity (ibid.: 156). How do they live their ethnicity? According to Crispino, this would entail the "celebration of feasts and ceremonial occasions, socializing, . . . organizational participation," and "practicing ethnicity" within the context of the family and peer group. These are the working-class ethnics, the "visible ethnics," who "tend to congregate in their traditional central city neighborhoods where their still somewhat distinctive life styles and institutions provide evidence to the rest of society that ethnicity is not dead. Their residential clustering means the possibility of conflict over turf and jobs with other, more recent arrivals in the city mainly blacks and Hispanics" (ibid.).

Crispino describes a second form of ethnicity, the "New Ethnicity," which, for him, exists on the non-behavioral level. People who express the new ethnicity preserve "sentimental attitudes toward their traditional culture" but do not adhere to "old ethnic practices" (ibid.: 158). This is in essence what Gans has called "symbolic ethnicity." For Chrispino, this form of ethnic identity is somewhat superficial and may be more appropriately "termed a 'label' rather than an 'identity'." Furthermore, "ethnicity and ethnic identification are particularly subject to exogenous influences and may be expected to wax and wane as external circumstances require" (ibid.: 159).

Ethnicity is more than merely an awareness or a sense of identity. There are behaviorial, organizational, and symbolic dimensions to ethnicity which vary with segments of the ethnic population. The class assimilationists make assumptions about the ethnic process in which they promulgate a particular view, i.e., a unilateral direction of change from a lower class immigrant population to a middle-class (preferably upper middle-class) population with virtually little or no ethnic accoutrements in any form. At best, the middle class population of whichever ethnic background may express some sense of ethnic identity in a variety of symbolic ways. Even the waxing and waning of ethnicity that Crispino alludes to is part of an enduring yet ever changing ethnicity which is shaped by both endogenous and exogenous forces and circumstances, each affecting the other, leading to new forms and styles.

Questions concerning the dynamics of Italian-American ethnicity are as equally important as those relating to issues of class. Language is generally viewed as an important aspect of ethnicity, e.g., whether one speaks Italian or English. Within the Italian-American population as a whole there is considerable variation not only in the Italian spoken but in the combinations of Italian and English and in the variations of English as well. The language styles of the Italian immigrants adapted to, and had an affect on, the emerging English-speaking styles of the second generation, which in turn affected the third generation, etc. The vernacular pronounciation of English words such as "ask" and "take," and casual speech patterns in general suggests that the ethnic process is evident in how groups of Italian-Americans speak English.

Beyond language, there are aspects of cuisine, including the socio-cultural context of eating — emphasis on family meals and holiday celebrations — which are part of the subculture of the Italian-Americans. Many Italian-Americans place a great deal of importance on life cycle, liturgical, and calendrical events such as: baptism, communion, confirmation, marriage, funeral ritual, Easter, Christmas, saints' days, birthdays, anniversaries of marriages, and anniversaries of deaths.

Feasts and street festivals — combining old and new characteristics — continue to provide an important dimension to a perduring Italian-American ethnicity. Despite the fact that many old neighborhoods change and feasts honoring the Madonna or a patron saint are discontinued, similar religious and secular festivities have been inaugurated in other neighborhoods which contain substantial numbers of Italian-Americans. A number of communities in the Bronx have begun or revived feasts. In June 1986, the Feast of the Grotto (Bronxwood and Mace Avenues) became the most recent of the Bronx feasts. On Long Island the parishioners of Saint Anthony's Church in Island Park began a festival for their saint less than a decade ago. Even neighborhoods such as Fords, New Jersey, with few Italian-Americans, find that feasts are an effective way of involving people in church rituals and in community activities. Moreover, these activities help raise money for the church. The Italian-Ameican feast complex consists of a socio-cultural inventory of traits which has undergone changes over the years but, nevertheless, continues to provide a paradigm for the emergence of variations of feasts and street festivals. It is yet another manifestation of the dynamic quality of ethnic phenomena.

In the social realm the ethnic process is manifested in gender roles and in interpersonal relationships within nuclear families, extended families, kindreds, peer groups, associations, and neighborhoods. It is generally expected that women will be mothers and family caretakers regardless of professional interests. Expectations are that males will be the primary providers and recipients of the nurturance of females (wives, mothers, sisters). It is also expected that children will remain with their family of orientation, the family into which they were born, until marriage. Frequently, married offspring, especially daughters, take up residence close to their parents. Siblings may buy homes or rent apartments on the same street or within the same neighborhood. Italian-Americans tend to live with one another in greater proportion than their general representation in the population would indicate. A more detailed discussion of the spatial clustering of Italian-Americans appears in a later section of this chapter.

Class assimilationists often assert that as ethnics move into the ranks of the middle class they often join associations that reflect their professional and personal interests rather than their ethnic interests. Or, if these organizations have some ethnic characteristics but the membership is primarily middle class, then the ethnic factor is somehow reduced. (Crispino 1980:162). It appears that for the class assimilationists, ethnicity is a fixed quantity comprising the social and cultural inventory of the immigrant and from which items can be subtracted. Nothing is said about adding to or about the changes in form and function of the traits of the social and cultural inventory. Still, the issue of associational ties must be given serious consideration in any discussion of enduring ethnicity.

Some people in Monte Carmelo join hometown clubs; others become members of social clubs and, in some instances, there are those who belong to both types of organizations. More recently, a number of Monte Carmelesi have come together to organize the Italian-American Cultural Society of the Bronx (IACSB). Although there may be fewer professionals in hometown associations than in IACSB, both associations have the sort of interests and objectives which are expressive of variant forms of Italian-American ethnicity. There are, in addition, numerous organizations that are specifially oriented toward the political and economic preservation of Italian-American hegemony in the community.

County, regional, and national Italian-American organizations are plentiful. In the New York metropolitan area there are hundreds of social, educational, artistic, political, recreational, hometown, cultural heritage, welfare, and other types of Italian-American associations. Among the many local and regional organizations are the following: Americans of Italian Heritage, American Italian Historical Association, American Italian Cultural and Literary Round Table, America-Italy Society, American Committee on Italian Migration, Association of Student and Professional Italian-Americans, Forum of Italian-American Educators, FIERI (an Italian-American youth organization), Italian-American Federation of Greater New York, Italian Heritage and Culture Committee of the Bronx and Westchester, Italian Heritage and Culture Committee of New York City, The Coalition of Italo-American Associations, The Columbus Citizens Foundations. There are, in addition, various national organizations such as the National Italian-American Foundation (NIAF), the National Organization of Italian-American Women, and the Sons of Italy. A number of the national associations, such as NIAF and the Sons of Italy, have local chapters.

A significant proportion of the organizations listed above consist of middle class Italian-Americans, many of whom would fit into Gans' category of "upper middle class professional." These associations — along with the many others representing a wide range of ethnic types within the Italian-American population — are a constant reminder of the viability and changing styles of Italian-American ethnicity.

Another protagonist of the class assimilationists thesis is Richard Alba who views the ethnicity of the Italian-American population as entering a "twilight stage." At the very outset he states in his recent book, *Italian Americans*, that he intends "to place assimilation in the inner circle of concern for the study of ethnicity" (Alba 1985: viii). According to his perception of the data

Italian Americans (and indeed other white ethnic groups) are rapidly converging with majority Americans. This means, first of all, that both are becoming alike in the important matters of social standing as well as those of culture. It means also that different ethnic origins no longer provide any serious impediment to social relations, including those of the most intimate and enduring kind, as the rising tide of intermarriage will indicate (ibid.).

Alba also notes that "the key forces that have propelled the process of convergence are *structural* and include the transformation of the occupational structure in the urban North, the residential dispersion to the suburbs, and the timely demographic shift to the second and now to the third generation" (ibid.). Alba does caution us that one should not accept this to mean "that assimilation is everywhere and for every group inevitable, but rather that it is brought about by a particular conjunction of circumstances" (ibid.). For Alba, intermarriage and social mobility are primary indices of structural assimilation which, in turn, "implies a dampening of cultural differences, a necessary precondition, and also of ethnic identity" (ibid.: 16). He views ethnicity for the descendants of European immigrants of the nineteenth and early twentieth centuries as "entering a kind of twilight state," a stage which may very well last "forever" (ibid.).

Somewhat melodramatically, Alba poses the question: "What is to be the fate of ethnic groups — will they endure as permanent features of the American landscape, or will they fade gradually into the background as a result of assimilation?" (ibid.: 2). Perhaps a more compelling question would be: How do ethnic populations adapt to changing social, cultural, and physical environments? Class assimilationists assume unidirectional changes and appear to hold relatively static views of ethnic cultures and societies. Italian-Americans, regardless of whether one views them as working class, lower middle-class, middle class, or upper class, display a considerable amount of intra-ethnic variation. The cultural styles of class groupings are in large measure shaped by the ethnic subcultures of its membership. Furthermore, class assimilationists also maintain a somewhat static view of class in that they assume a homogeneity of style based on class membership. Class assimilationists operate under the premise that there is a uniformity of convergence to American society. Such an assumption is singularly teleological. It is also indicative, to my way of thinking, of an underlying ideological stance encompassing the view that American society is a relatively open system allowing individuals of different ethnic backgrounds access to the material and social rewards which are the concomitants of upward mobility. Ethnic status, on the other hand, is viewed as an "impediment" to economic and social mobility.

Alba states that "Italian-Americans stand on the verge of the twilight of their ethnicity" (ibid.: 159). Either his prescience is extraordinary, or his use of metaphor is misleading.

Twilight appears an accurate metaphor for a stage when ethnic differences remain visible but only faintly so, when ethnic forms can be perceived only in vague outline. The twilight metaphor acknowledges that ethnicity has not entirely disappeared ... but at the same time, it captures the reality that ethnicity is nonetheless steadily receding. The twilight metaphor also allows for the occasional flare-ups of ethnic feelings and conflicts that give the illusion that ethnicity is reviving, but are little more than flickers in the fading light (ibid.).

"Twilight" as a metaphor does not convey an accurate image of Italian-American ethnicity. Twilight is an integral part of both day and night, a segment of a changing whole. Italian-Americans are a changing ethnic population and these changes reflect inner-directed and outer-directed processes. A twilight metaphor is a negation of the dynamic quality of socio-cultural phenomena. Class assimilationists have a static view of ethnicity in that they expect the social and cultural characteristics of the immigrant generation to be perpetuated in subsequent generations in order for the group to be considered a bonafide ethnic population. Changes in form and function occur and are shaped by previous historical contexts. Undoubtedly, Italian-Americans of the second and third generations are different from first-generation Italian-Americans. However, the distinctiveness of the differences as compared with, for example, the distinctiveness of the differences that characterize Irish-Americans or Polish-Americans of comparable generations are in part, at least, the result of a distinctive historical experience. The twilight does not last forever as Alba should have recognized in his use of metaphor, since twilight is part of the diurnal-nocturnal cyclical process which, like ethnicity, is a dynamic phenomenon.

Stephen Steinberg (1981) in his book, *Ethnic Myth*, also argues for the pro-class position. He writes: "Where the class theory differs from the cultural theory (or ethnic theory) is in its emphasis on the primacy of class factors" (132). Consequently, according to Steinberg's view, the ethnic characteristics of a particular population are a function of its class position in the society. Individuals of the lower class stratum, for example, would evidence "most authentically," to use his phrase, ethnic patterns as compared with those of the middle and upper strata. The genuine ethnics, therefore, are members of the lower class. These are the individuals whose social mobility has been stifled by their marginal economic position. Upward mobility diminishes ethnicity. It would be interesting to speculate whether downward mobility recreates the pristine ethnic state.

More than twenty years ago in *Assimilation in American Life* (1964), Milton Gordon clearly recognized the relationship between ethnicity and social class. He coined the word *ethclass* to describe "the subsociety created by the intersection of the vertical stratifications of ethnicity with the horizontal stratifications of social class" (51). Although Gordon's view of an ethnic group, a people with a sense of common identity, is somewhat limited, he nevertheless acknowledges the relevance of the ethnic factor in the structural dimensions of a society. Ethnicity is no less important in its effect on the behavioral modes of individuals.

The Monte Carmelesi and Italian-Americans in general constitute a population demonstrating both intra-ethnic variations and inter-class similarities. In arguing that ethnicity dims as upward mobility increases, the class assimilationists fail to discern the dynamic qualities of ethnic phenomena.

## THE SPATIAL DIMENSION OF ITALIAN-AMERICAN ETHNICITY

It is generally recognized that spatial contiguity enhances ethnic solidarity, and despite the claims of the class assimilationists who argue that Italian-Americans are losing their ethnic qualities but gaining in class, Italian-Americans have demonstrated a preference for living in neighborhoods where their co-ethnics comprise either majorities or significant proportions of the population. Data from census tracts (census "neighborhoods") clearly demonstrate the clustering propensity of Italian-Americans. Many of the neighborhoods listed below are not areas of original settlement and include substantial members of third- and fourth-generation Italian-

Americans. Furthermore, there are numbers of Italian-Americans of mixed ancestry in a high percentage of the neighborhoods.

A concentration of Italian-Americans in census neighborhoods such as Monte Carmelo, Morris Park, Villa Avenue, Throgs Neck, Pelham Bay, Eastchester Road, and Country Club in The Bronx; Silver Lake (Harrison), Eastchester, and sections of Yonkers in Westchester County; Island Park, Deer Park, Lindenhurst, and Oyster Bay in Nassau and Suffolk Counties; Bensonhurst, Sheepshead Bay, and Mill Basin in Brooklyn; Astoria, Corona, and Woodhaven in Queens suggests that kinship, friendship, and associational ties are operative. Often these ties are crucial in determining where people will move. A recently married woman from Monte Carmelo rents an apartment near a sister who lives in Pelham Bay. A family that emigrated from Italy in the late sixties and settled in Monte Carmelo buys a house near a *paesano* in the Eastchester Road section. Not only do intra-ethnic social ties continue to play an important role in the lives of the Italian-Americans living in these census neighborhoods but, in addition, relatively distincitve cultural patterns identify them as an ethnic population. What follows is an enumeration of census tracts with significant numbers of Italian-Americans.[1] The geographic region encompasses New York City, Long Island, and areas of New Jersey and lower New York State.

Since Monte Carmelo is located in the Bronx, it would be appropriate to begin with that borough. There are close to 132,000 Italian-Americans living in the Bronx, and as a group they make up 11.27 percent of the borough population. In 58 of the census tracts Italian-Americans comprise 25 percent or more of the total population, and in 43 of the census tracts they account for 40 percent of the population. There are twelve census tracts where Italian-Americans constitute 60 percent and above of the area's population. The general figures for the Bronx as a whole indicate that nearly 60 percent of the Italian-Americans live in 20.7 percent of the census tracts.

Since World War II, there has been a large outflow of Italian-Americans from Manhattan. It is the borough with the smallest number of Italian-Americans, 72,441, a mere 5 percent of Manhattan's population. Still, there are 12 census tracts in which Italian-Americans comprise 15 percent or better of the population, three times their representation of the borough population. In 6 of these census tracts they constitute 21 percent to 28.4 percent of the area inhabitants. What also has to be considered is that the distribution of the Italian-American population in a census tract is no necessrily uniform. In East Harlem, which at one time house as many as 90,000 Italian-Americans, the few thousand that are still living there may be found on certain blocks or in clusters of buildings on particular blocks. A clustering pattern within census tracts is also evident in Monte Carmelo.

The largest number of the city's Italian-Americans, 361,450, live in Brooklyn where they comprise 16.2 percent of the borough population. In 160 of the 790 census tracts, Italian-Americans constitute better than 30 percent of the people, and in 81 of the census tracts they make up more than 50 percent of the population. There are 39 census tracts in which they represnet 70 to 90 percent of the total number of inhabitants. For the borough as a whole, 56 percent of the Italian-Americans live in 20.3 percent of the census tracts.

Nearly 305,000 Italian-Americans, 16 percent of the borough population, live in Queens. In 114 of the 658 census tracts they constitute 30 percent or more of the residents, and in 54 of the census tracts they account for 40 to 70 percent of the people. A total of 104,239 Italian-Americans live in 18.5 percent of the borough's census tracts.

Of the five boroughs of New York City, Staten Island has the highest proportion of Italian-Americans, 38.2 percent. In 15 of the 101 census tracts, Italian-Americans form 50 percent or more of the population. Overall, 83 percent of the Italian-Americans living in Staten Island are concentrated in 49 of the 101 census tracts.

There are 306,226 Italian-Americans living in Nassau County (Long Island), 23.2 percent of the population. In a number of county units they constitute more than 30 percent of the residents: Bethpage, 33 percent; East Massapequa, 30.8 percent; Elmont, 41.5 percent; Franklin Square, 42.3 percent; Glen Cove City, 31.2 percent; South Farmingdale, 34.4 percent; Valley Stream Village, 38 percent; and West Hempstead, 31.6 percent.

One out of every four residents of Suffolk County (Long Island) is an Italian-American. In 20 of the 46 county units they comprise 30 percent or more of the population.[2]

It should be noted that the county units — for both Nassau and Suffolk — are broken down into census tracts and the clustering effect is more pronounced in some of the tracts, reflecting a higher percentage than the figure for the entire county unit would indicate.

In West Babylon (Suffolk County), for example, Italian-Americans constitute 40 percent or more of the residents in 4 of the 9 census tracts. In one particular census tract neighborhood, they make up 57 percent of the population. The clustering effect is also apparent in county units where the percentage of Italian-Americans is considerably lower than the percentage for the county as a whole. In Wyandanch (Suffolk County), 11.1 percent of the residents are Italian-Americans. Yet 92.4 percent of them live in 2 of the 5 census tracts. Similarly, in Freeport Village (Nassau County) where Italian-Americans make up 10.5 percent of the inhabitants, 70 percent of them live in 3 of the 8 census tracts.

The clustering of Italian-Americans in census tract neighborhoods is also evident in the suburbs of Westchester, Rockland, and Putnam Counties. In one of the census tracts of Suffern Village (Rockland County), they comprise 31.7 percent of the population. Italian-Americans are heavily represented in Eastchester (Westchester County) where the number in 4 of the 5 census tracts exceeds 30 percent, and in 2 of the census tracts they constitute more than 40 percent of the residents. Half of the census tracts of Harrison Village have 50 percent to 60 percent Italian-American residents. In 2 of the 4 census tracts that make up Mamaroneck Village (Westchester County), Italian-Americans number more than 42 percent of the population. The proportion of Italian-Americans living in Port Chester is well above their 24.3 percent representation in Westchester County. Furthermore, in 4 of 5 census tracts, they account for 35 percent to 54 percent of the Port Chester residents.

For many years, Yonkers attracted Italian-Americans seeking inexpensive housing in "good neighborhoods." This is reflected in their distribution in the census tracts. Once again the cluster effect is clearly discernable. In 39 percent of the tracts, for example, Italian-Americans constitute from 35 percent to 59 percent of the inhabitants. They account for more than 50 percent of the population in 4 census tracts. Another area of Westchester County in which Italian-Americans have settled is Mount Vernon. Their distribution in 5 of the census tracts ranges from 38 percent to 50 percent of the total.

The clustering of Italian-Americans occurs in the suburbs of Putnam County (New York State) and northern New Jersey. In 5 of the census tracts of Putnam County, they represent from 30 percent to 38 percent of the residents. The 209,559 Italian-Americans living in Bergen County, New Jersey, comprise nearly 25 percent of the county's population. They exceed this proportion in 48 of the 154 census tracts, and in 15 census tracts they account for more than 40 percent of the inhabitants. Approximately 50 percent of Bergen County's Italian-Americans live in 33 percent of the census tracts. A general assessment of the census tract data indicating areas of residence of more than 2,100,000 Italian-Americans (including over 570,000 of mixed ancestry) who live in New York City and the surrounding suburbs, evidences a cluster pattern of settlement. A more careful study of block segments indicates high concentrations of Italian-Americans within specific areas of the census tracts. This is evident not only in Monte Carmelo which has had a long history as an ethnic neighborhood, but also in places like Oceanside, one of Long Island's more affluent communities, where, in recent years, Italian-Americans have settled in increasing numbers. This preference for co-ethnics which is manifested in the clustering of Italian-Americans in particular neighborhoods demonstrates that Italian-American ethnicity is far from "dimming."

## THE MAFIA IMAGE

A Monte Carmeleso, a student at one of the CUNY senior colleges, wrote a paper on the influence of the mafia in Monte Carmelo. In conversations with me, he stated that the information in the paper was deliberately tailored to meet the expectations of the instructor who was convinced that neighborhoods with large numbers of Italian-Americans were mafia infested. The stereotype proved salutary for the young man who received a good grade. For his co-ethnics, however, it has been a baneful image, largely exploited by the media, and damaging in its consequences for an entire ethnic population.

Paradoxically, Monte Carmelo appears to be relatively crime free, if one were to believe media portrayals, and simultaneously, mafia dominated. Some may argue that *it is crime free* precisely because it is mafia controlled. Neither is an accurate appraisal of the realities of life in Monte Carmelo.

Within the past four and one-half years there have been six homicides within the community. In addition, there have been robberies, burglaries, and assaults. Gambling, of course, continues to be the most popular non-violent crime in the neighborhood. The assertion that Monte Carmelo is a safe neighborhood is primarily a promotional gimmick to encourage people to visit and to shop. One wonders why the safe environment has not encouraged many of the merchants to live in the neighborhood. The Merchant Association's active campaign to foster a safe community image creates a distorted view of life in Monte Carmelo. Crimes do occur: people are killed; storekeepers are held up; cars are vandalized; and apartments are burglarized.

It is not my intention to create the impression that Monte Carmelo is a crime-ridden neighborhood. To do so would be as inaccurate as to unequivocably affirm that it is a "safe" community. A more balanced view requires that one recognize that crimes are committed and at a higher frequency than the expectations conveyed by newspaper articles and statements made by community spokespeople.

Perhaps people can be persuaded that Monte Carmelo is a relatively crimefree neighborhood. However, it would be virtually impossible to dissuade them that it is mafia free. Whether one discusses Monte Carmelo, Morris Park, Country Club, Throgs Neck, Whitestone, Canarsie, Mill Basin, Eastchester, or any of the other Italian-American communities throughout the New York metropolitan region, the specter of the mafia continues to haunt the Italian-American population. The mafia image in various guises — the black hand, *cosa nostra* (our thing), the syndicate, and the mob — has evolved into a distinctive marker of Italian-American ethnicity. It has become part of the folk tradition of American society to view the mafia as an Italian and an Italian-American phenomenon. If one were to gratuitously accept the information disseminated in newspapers, magazines, films, television programs, and books, the impression would be that for nearly a century Italian-Americans have emerged as the most powerful, pervasive, violent, and economically successful criminals in the United States. And they have achieved this notoriety, according to the popular view, through a cartelike structure called the mafia.

Monte Carmelo has not escaped the mafia stigma. If someone in the community had been involved in a number of bank robberies, few would acknowledge that these crimes were committed by a single individual acting on his own. Similarly, a homicide invariably means that someone has been eliminated by the mob. Criminal behavior on the part of Monte Carmelesi, or on the part of Italian-Americans in general, is usually interpreted to be mafia related. For tens of millions of people the mafia concept has come to mean an Italian-American criminal organization with historical ties to southern Italy. The image itself generates a transcendental sense of awe about an organization which is believed to be omnipotent. The mystical quality of the mafia, however, is in sharp contrast to the profane occurrences of criminal life as it is presented in the media: the execution of *capos* (heads of "families") or underbosses whose blood-stained bodies appear on the front pages of newspapers; arrests and trials of important mob figures with photos and nicknames; and the interminable accounts of family structures, leadership rivalries, and interfamily conflicts. More recently there has been a considerable amount of interest in a suprafamily organization, the "commission."

No such organization orchestrates the criminal activities in Monte Carmelo. The gambling racket is probably the most effectively organized illegal activity in the community. Still, it doesn't necessarily follow that merely because a criminal activity is organized, it warrants a mafia label. This distorted image persists because two unjustified assumptions are made: all organized crime is mafia related; and mafia is defined in terms of Italian-American ethnicity. This is the sort of imagery that has afflicted not only the Monte Carmelesi, but all Italian-Americans.

## NOTES

1. Information on single and multiple foreign ancestry has been culled from the *United States Census of Population: 1980, General Characteristics of Persons* (U.S. Bureau of the Census 1980). Unless otherwise stated, the ethnic category "Italian-American" includes both single ancestry and multiple foreign ancestry.
2. The list of units and the percentage of Italian-Americans includes the following: Centereach, 31.7 percent; Commack, 30.5 percent; Copiague, 38.2 percent; Deer Park, 41.7 percent; Elwood, 30.5 percent; Farmingville, 33.5 percent; Hauppauge, 34.2 percent; Holbrook, 34.3 percent; Holtsville, 35.4 percent; Lake Ronkonkoma, 32.5 percent; Lindenhurst Village, 37.1 percent; Mastic, 32 percent; Nesconset, 30.7 percent; North Babylon, 38.2 percent; North Lindenhurst, 40.2 percent; Seldon, 38.6 percent; Shirley, 40.1 percent; Smithtown, 31 percent; West Babylon, 37.4 percent; and West Islip, 32.5 percent.

# Epilogue

It's a muggy Sunday morning in Monte Carmelo. The church bells have a muffled sound because of the thick, misty air blanketing the area. Later today the procession in honor of Our Lady of Mount Carmel will work its way through the streets of the enclave. New decorations commemorating the eightieth anniversary of the church form a resplendent canopy above the few booths set up for the feast.

The gloominess of the day further adds to a sense of loss as one walks along Main Street listening to the pealing bells and watching the people climbing the steps of the church in order to participate in the celebration of the High Mass. Eighty years ago Monte Carmelesi crowded into a small storefront church to hear an Italian priest from Milan preach to them about Jesus and the Madonna and to tell them about how one day the storefront will be transformed into a magnificent Romanesque structure where thousands of people will worship, receive communion, be confirmed, be married, baptize their children, and have their bodies blessed by the Church when they die.

Eleven years later the church bells of Our Lady of Mount Carmel sounded for the first time as a huge throng gathered to commemorate its inaugural. In the sixty-nine years that followed, the church has stood as the implacable bastion of *Italianita* in the community, reaching out to embrace the thousands of emigrants who came from the towns of southern Italy and large numbers of Italian-Americans from various parts of New York City who settled there. It evolved into the quintessential collective symbol of Italian-American ethnicity.

The scenario that one is confronted with on this oppressive Sunday morning contrasts with other Sunday mornings in mid-July when booths filled the streets and people strolled along Main Street anxiously awaiting the brilliant display of fireworks. The Feast of Our Lady Of Mount Carmel is no longer what it used to be. Within the past few years the changes have been particularly striking. During the 1985 feast there were about a dozen booths, a figure considerably lower than in previous years. This year there are seven booths, the lowest number I have ever observed. Even the procession is considerably smaller than in previous years. The high humidity and the threat of rain may have discouraged many from participating. Still, the drastic decline in the number of booths and a much smaller area for *festa*-related activities are signs that the commercial interests find the secular activities less profitable.

Like the Feast of Our Lady of Mount Carmel, the community has also changed. Following the route of the procession, I stroll the streets of the enclave where one finds the highest concentration of Italian-Americans and I see different faces representing a variety of ethnic groups. There are blocks where Italian-Americans live on one side of the street and Blacks and Puerto Ricans on the other. There are Latin Americans, Asians, Albanians, Yugoslavians, and Irish interspersed with Italian-Americans. As I pass the Market Street Park, I notice a small group of Hispanics playing basketball. Although the park continues to be controlled by Italian-Americans, there has been some sharing of recreational space with other ethnic groups. Nevertheless, the Italian and American flags painted on the handball walls are compelling reminders of proprietorship not only of the handball courts, but of the park and the enclave itself.

Turning east on Main Street from Market Street, I make my way back to the church. Walking along Main Street, I become more immersed in the Italian-American quality of the neighborhood with its cafés, bakeries, bread stores, pizzerias, pork stores, and the people — some hanging out or exchanging a few pleasantries; others shopping; and those, like me, leisurely strolling alongside the procession.

As the procession proceeds eastward on Main Street, I reflect on the future of the community. For most of the people that I have spoken to in the past four and half years, Monte Carmelo has changed for the "worse" and will continue to deteriorate. There are some, especially a number of the merchants and others who have a stake in maintaining Italian-American economic and political domination of the neighborhood, who claim to see a glimmer of an ethnic resurgence. Great efforts have been made both to stem the exodus of Italian-Americans and to entice outsiders — Italian-Americans and other Whites — to move in. My impressions are that the outflow rate of Italian-Americans from the community has dropped and there has been a minuscule inflow. Certainly, the mass exodus of the late sixties and seventies has diminished considerably in recent years.

Reviewing the situation on my particular block for the past three years, there has been very little change in the number of Italian-American families. One of my neighbor's married daughters who lived in the apartment below him moved to New Jersey. She was replaced by another married daughter who previously lived in Yonkers. In a number of years she probably will buy a house in suburbia, perhaps near her sister, and her father will carefully select his next renter. This neighborhood tenaciousness of a segment of the Italian-American population is tied to private house ownership. Most of the Italian-Americans who continue to live in Monte Carmelo, while their co-ethnics leave, own their own homes. Capitalizing on this tradition, community leaders initiated a program of subsidized housing which resulted in the construction of approximately fifty private houses. Nearly all of them have been purchased by Italian-Americans. Recent efforts to contain the movement of Italian-Americans out of Monte Carmelo have met with some success.

Demographic changes notwithstanding, Monte Carmelo continues to function as a mecca of Italian-American ethnicity. There are those who periodically make pilgrimages to the community to reaffirm their sense of identity and to participate in its secular and religious ceremonial life. As I approach the church, I am reminded of another place, another time, another Our Lady of Mount Carmel. It was July 1946, nearly a year after World War II had ended. My mother had made special promises to various saints and to Our Lady of Mount Carmel that if my older brother returned safely from the battlefields of Europe, she would maintain a special devotion to each of them by votive offerings, by visiting their churches, and by participating in the rituals of the *festa*. It was in fulfillment of a *voto* (vow) that my parents accompanied by their young son travelled to 115th Street and Pleasant Avenue to visit the Church of Our Lady of Mount Carmel, the cynosure of the Italian-American community of East Harlem for more than forty years. My mother removed her shoes to climb the steps of the church. As I held her shoes, she entered the church and walked down the center aisle until she reached the statue of the Madonna, and then in a gesture of profound gratitude, she fell to her knees. Her tears and prayers mingled in a litany of thanksgiving. The poignancy of this act of a grateful mother can be more fully appreciated in view of the fact that three of her five sons died in early childhood. All of her nine daughters survived.

Forty years later, the Madonna, perched on a stand, is still pulled through a few of the streets of East Harlem. Hundreds of Italian-Americans from different parts of the city, from suburbia, and from nearby states come to participate in the procession. There are those who petition Our Lady of Mount Carmel for special favors; others return to make good on old promises. At one time East Harlem, with its 90,000 Italian-Americans, was the largest Italian-American community in the United States. Now the population is scarcely 2 percent of what it had been.

These are some of my thoughts as I pause outside the church and join the group that gathers to watch as the statue of the Madonna is being carried into the church. I think about East Harlem and Monte Carmelo, two communities in neighboring boroughs with the same patroness. The Bronx community is nearly a century old whereas the Italian settlement of East Harlem began about 115 years ago. There were three times the number of Italian-Americans living in East Harlem as compared with Monte Carmelo during their respective "Golden Ages."

The first significant inflow of non-Italian-Americans into East Harlem began about fifty-five years after Italian-Americans originally settled in the area. In Monte Carmelo this occurred about sixty years after the first settlement. Presently the Italian-American population of my neighborhood is approximately thirty percent of what it had been in its prime. Will the number decrease in the next fifteen to twenty years? Will the church and the *festa*, a handful of merchants and restaurateurs, and a thousand or so middle-aged and elderly Italian-Americans comprise the vestige of an Italian-American community in the early years of the twenty-first century?

I reflect on these questions as the Madonna is being carried into the church. The questions relate to issues concerning the viability of the more traditional ethnic neighborhoods. East Harlem is a remnant of what was once the largest Italian-American community in the country. The North End, an old Italian-American community in Boston, is succumbing to the "yuppie" influence. Monte Carmelo, a large Italian-American community a few decades ago, has become an enclave in a multi-ethnic neighborhood.

It seems to me that different questions ought to be asked and other issues explored. What should concern us are queries regarding the dynamics of ethnicity, that is ethnicity as an on-going process. Traditional Italian-American communities are integral parts of the general history of an entire ethnic population. Moreover, these traditional communities are not static social and cultural phenomena. One can discern evidence of change in the differences manifested in a range of Italian-American types. In addition, these communities become focal points for other Italian-Americans living in other communities who visit or who view them as collective expressions of their own ethnicity. For large numbers of Italian-Americans distributed in neighborhoods of the Bronx, Westchester County, New Jersey, and in other areas, Monte Carmelo is perceived to be a remnant of a pristine ethnic essence. Its significance transcends the spatial boundaries of the enclave in that it links together a wide range of Italian-American types. However small the enclave becomes, it will continue to function as a mecca of *Italianita*. As such, it serves as a conduit of ethnic consciousness for large numbers of Italian-Americans throughout the metropolitan area, many of whom live in neighborhoods with high concentrations of their co-ethnics. If the structural from of the community holds together, and I think it will, Monte Carmelo should survive as an Italian-American enclave for many years.

When I enter the church I am somewhat surprised to see so many people waiting inside. Given the number of people participating in the procession, I had expected a smaller turn out. Some stare in awe as the statue is carried down the center aisle, some whisper prayers of thanksgiving and petition, and there are others engaged in conversations who appear to be completely oblivious to the proceedings.

The dozens of conversations make it difficult for those of us in the back of the church to follow the service. The pastor, dressed in the red cassock of a monsignor, begins the homily by apprising the people that devotion to the Madonna is a way of serving God and the Church. As the pastor speaks, I realize that he is addressing us in English. Later he repeats the message in Italian. I am witnessing a bilingual service in which English takes precedence over Italian. One of the most traditional practices in the community, the Feast of Our Lady of Mount Carmel, is responding to changing circumstances. Unlike the previous pastors, he appears to be more American oriented than Italian oriented. Interestingly the ethnic orientation of the pastor is compatible with that of the economic and political leaders of Monte Carmelo.

As the pastor addresses the congregation in Italian, I notice that some of the people become more attentive while others find it difficult to understand. The hundreds of people in the church, like the Monte Carmelesi and Italian-Americans in general, manifest a variety of socio-cultural types which together comprise an ethnic population. In particular situations and in particular places, these differences are mediated through collective expressions of unity. Our Lady of Mount Carmel is one such symbol of Italian-American ethnicity. Resting on a stand at the front of the church, the statue of the Madonna faces the people and the streets of Monte Carmelo. And the streets of Monte Carmelo extend far beyond the boundaries of the enclave.

# Bibliography

Alba, Richard. 1985. *Italian Americans.* Englewood Cliffs, N.J.: Prentice-Hall, Inc.

Barth, Fredrik. 1969. *Ethnic Groups and Boundaries.* Boston: Little, Brown and Company.

Bartlett, Kim. 1977. *The Finest Kind.* New York: W.W. Norton and Company Inc.

Bianco, Carla. 1974. *The Two Rosetos.* Bloomington: Indiana University Press.

Caroli, Betty B., Robert F. Harney, and Lydio F. Tomasi, eds. 1978. *The Italian Immigrant Woman in North America.* Toronto: The Multicultural History Society of Ontario.

Castile, George P., and Gilbert Kushner, eds. 1981. *Persistent Peoples.* Tucson: University of Arizona Press.

Cinel, Dino. 1982. *From Italy to San Francisco.* Stanford: Stanford University Press.

Cook, Harry T. 1913. *The Borough of the Bronx, 1639–1913.* New York: By the Author.

Coser, Lewis. 1966. *The Functions of Social Conflict.* New York: The Free Press.

Covello, Leonard. 1958. *The Heart is the Teacher.* New York: McGraw-Hill Book Company.

—. 1967. *The Social Background of the Italian American School Child.* Leiden: E.J. Brill.

Crispino, James A. 1980. *The Assimilation of Ethnic Groups: The Italian Case.* Staten Island, N.Y.: Center for Migration Studies.

DeConde, A. 1971. *Half Bitter, Half Sweet: An Excursion into Italian American History.* New York: Charles Scribner's Sons.

D'Erasmo, Rocky. 1978. *Fordham Was a Town.* New York: By the Author.

Di Donato, Pietro. 1937. *Christ in Concrete.* New York: The Bobbs-Merill Company.

Di Leonardo, Micaela. 1984. *The Varieties of Ethnic Experience.* Ithaca: Cornell University Press.

English, Bella. "A Bronx area one of USA's 'safest'." *New York Daily News*, September 9, 1983, p. 5.

Foerster, Robert F. 1968. *The Italian Emigration of Our Times.* New York: Russell and Russell.

Gambino, Richard. 1974. *Blood of My Blood: The Dilemma of Italian Americans.* Garden City, N.Y.: Doubleday and Company.

Gans, Herbert J. 1982. *The Urban Villagers.* Updated and expanded edition. New York: The Free Press.

Glazer, Nathan, and Daniel P. Moynihan, eds., 1975. *Ethnicity.* Cambridge, Mass: Harvard University Press.

—. 1983. *Beyond the Melting Pot.* Cambridge, Mass: M.I.T. Press.

—. *Golden Jubilee of Our Lady of Mount Carmel, 1906–1956.* 1956. New York: Victory Print, Inc.

Gordon, Milton M. 1964. *Assimilation in American Life.* New York: Oxford University Press.

Greeley, Andrew M. 1974. *Ethnicity in the United States*. New York: Wiley.

Horowitz, Donald L. 1985. *Ethnic Groups in Conflict*. Berkeley and Los Angeles: University of California Press.

Iorizzo, Luciano J., and Salvatore Mondello. 1980. *The Italian Americans*. New York: Twayne Publishers.

James, George. "For the Bronx, A New Image Is a Tough Sell." *New York Times*, June 10, 1986, sec. B, p. 1.

Keyes, Charles, ed. 1979. *Ethnic Adaptation and Identity*. Philadelphia: ISHI.

LaRuffa, Anthony, ed. 1982. "Italians in the United States: Some Issues and Problems. *Ethnic Groups: An Inernational Periodical of Ethnic Studies* 4(3).

—. In press. "Conflict and the Development of an Italian-American Enclave in the Bronx." In *The Anthropology of War and Peace: Conflict, Diplomacy, and the Global System*, Mario D. Zamora and Anthony L. LaRuffa, editors. Marawi City, The Philippines: St. Mary's College and the Southern Philippine Center for Peace Studies, Mindanao State University.

Lewis, John. "Belmont remains an Italian oasis." *New York Daily News*. March 14, 1982, sec. MB, p. 3.

LoPreato, Joseph. 1970. *Italian-Americans*. New York: Random House.

Mangano, Antonio. 1975. *Italians in the City*. New York: Arno Press.

Mangione, Jerre. 1942. *Mount Allegro*. Boston: Houghton Mifflin Company.

Maraspino, A.L. 1968. *The Study of an Italian Village*. The Hague: Mouton and Co.

Merchants Association. n.d. *Guide to Monte Carmelo*. New York.

Moses, Peter. "They Walked Unafraid." *New York Post*. July 2, 1985. p. 14.

Moss, Leonard. 1977. "The Family in Southern Italy: Yesterday and Today." In *The United States and Italy: The First Two Hundred Years*, Humbert S. Nelli, editor. New York: The American Italian Historical Association, pp. 185–191.

Nelli, Humbert S. 1970. *Italians in Chicago, 1880–1930: A Study in Ethnic Mobility*. New York: Oxford University Press.

—. 1976. *The Business of Crime*. Chicago: The University of Chicago Press.

Newman, Jill. "What Has Happened To America's Safest Cities?" *Good Housekeeping*. May 1985, p. 340.

Orsi, Robert. 1985. *The Madonna of 115th Street*. New Haven: Yale University Press.

Panunzio, Constantine M. 1921. *The Soul of an Immigrant*. New York: Macmillan.

Peroni, Peter A. 1979. *The Burg: An Italian American Community at Bay in Trenton*. Washington, D.C.: University Press of America, Inc.

Puzo, Mario. 1964. *The Fortunate Pilgrim*. Greenwich, Conn.: Fawcett Crest Books.

Smith, Dwight. 1975. *The Mafia Mystique*. New York: Basic Books.

Smith, Judith E. 1985. *Family Connections*. Albany: State University of New York Press.

Steinberg, Stephen. 1981. *The Ethnic Myth: Race, Ethnicity, and Class in America*. New York: Atheneum.

Suttles, Gerald D. 1968. *The Social Order of the Slum*. Chicago: The University of Chicago Press.

Tomasi, Lydio F., ed. 1977. *Perspectives in Italian Immigration and Ethnicity*. Staten Island, N.Y.: Center for Migration Studies.

—. 1985. *Italian Americans: New Perspectives in Italian Immigration and Ethnicity*. Staten Island, N.Y.: Center for Migration Studies.

U.S. Bureau of the Census. 1913. *Thirteenth Census of the United States, 1910. Population*, Vol. III. Washington, D.C.: Goverment Printing Office

——. 1921. *Fourteenth Census of the United States, 1920: Population*, Vol. III. Washington, D.C.: Government Printing Office.

——. 1931. *Fifteenth Census of the United States, 1930: Population*, Vol. III. Part 2. Washington, D.C.: U.S. Government Printing Office.

——. 1942. *Sixteenth Census of the United States, 1940: Population*, Vol. IV. Part 3. Washington, D.C.: U.S. Government Printing Office.

——. 1952. *United States Census of Population: 1950*, Vol. III. Characteristics of the Population, New York. Washington, D.C.: U.S. Government Printing Office.

——. 1963. *United States Census of Population: 1960*, General Characteristics of the Population. Washington, D.C.: U.S. Government Printing Office.

——. 1972. *United States Census of Population: 1970*, Social Characteristics of the Population. Washington, D.C.: U.S. Government Printing Office.

——. 1982. *United States Census of Population: 1980*, General Characteristics of Persons. Washington, D.C.: U.S. Government Printing Office.

Ware, Caroline. 1965. *Greenwich Village, 1920–1930*. New York: Harper and Row.

Wellisz, Christopher. "Bronx Neighborhood: 'One Big Family'." *New York Times.* September 14, 1983, sec. B, p. 1.

Whyte, William F. 1967. *Street Corner Society*. Chicago: University of Chicago Press.

Williams, Phyllis H. 1938. *South Italian Folkways in Europe and America*. New Haven: Yale University Press.

Yans-McLaughlin, Virginia. 1977. *Family and Community: Italian Immigration in Buffalo, 1880–1930*. Ithaca: Cornell University Press.

# INDEX

Alba, Richard, xvii n, 133, 134
Albanians, 20, 27, 55, 58, 91
    population statistics, 119-120
*Amici. See* Friends
Amulets, 11, 73
Apartments
    high-rise, 25, 38, 96, 100
    renovation of, 25, 38, 96-97, 100
    renting of, to Italian-Americans, 25,
        38, 96, 97, 101
    rents of, 33, 71, 73, 86
    for senior citizens, 96
Assimilation, xviii, 123-134, 135
*Assimilation in American Life* (Gordon),
    135
*Assimilation of Ethnic Groups: The Italian
    Case, The* (Crispino), 128-129
Associations
    community. *See* Organizations,
        community
    ethnicity and, 131-133
    hometown, 21, 101-103, 132

Baptism, 10, 46, 86, 110, 111
Barth, Fredrik, xviii n
Behavior, object-oriented versus person-
    oriented, 126-127
Blacks, 26, 27-28, 49
    classification of, 90-91
    household income of, 88, 89 *t*
    inter-ethnic conflict and, 19-20, 49,
        116
    occupations of, 89 *t*, 90
    population statistics, 19, 20, 119
    in public schools, 36, 49, 74
    as *stranieri*, 20, 23

Bookies, 35, 105, 106
Boys. *See* Males
Bridgeport, Connecticut, 128
Bronx (New York City)
    feasts in, new, 131
    Italian-American neighborhoods in, 3,
        18, 19, 122, 136
    Italian-American population statistics
        for, 136
    residential mobility and, 18, 19, 42,
        76
Bronx overall Development Corporation,
    99
Brooklyn (New York City)
    Italian-American neighborhoods in, 4,
        136
    Italian-American population statistics
        for, 137

Cafés, 21
Card playing, 102
    gambling and, 34, 104, 105-106
Castile, George P., xviii n
*Christ in Concrete* (Di Donato), 101-102
Church, Catholic. *See also* Our Lady of
    Mount Carmel Church
    criticisms of, 10, 46, 52, 56-57
    life cycle rituals of, 10, 46, 86, 110
    in southern Italy, 10
Church attendance, 46, 78, 82, 83, 85,
    86, 112-113
    ethnic orientation and, 22
    gender differences in, 8, 10, 67, 76
    in southern Italy, 8, 10
Church organizations and activities, 75,
    78, 80, 82, 85, 111, 113-114

153

Class, social. *See* Social class; Social
    mobility
Class assimilationist view, xviii, 124-134,
    135
Clubs, 34, 100-104. *See also* Hometown
    associations
    social, 34, 103-104, 132
Cognitive processes, 125-126
College education. *See* Education, college
*Comare*, 63, 91 n
    in southern Italy, 9
COMCO. *See* Council of Monte Carmelo
    Organizations
Communion, first holy, 10, 46, 86, 110
Community organizations. *See* Organiza-
    tions, community
*Comparaggio*, 64
    in southern Italy, 9
*Compare*, 63, 65, 91n
    in southern Italy, 9
Confirmation, 10, 46, 110
Conflict
    inter-ethnic, 19-20, 23, 27-28, 49, 58,
        74, 116
    inter-neighborhood, 28 n, 115
    intra-ethnic, 26, 28 n
Consumer goods, 127, 128
*Contadini*, 1, 2
Cook, Harry T., 17
Council of Monte Carmelo Organizations
    (COMCO), 25, 38, 97-100, 104
Covello, Leonard, 1, 2, 6, 7
Crime, 57-58, 59, 61, 62 n, 105, 109,
    139, 140. *See also* Gambling;
    Homicides; Violence
    image of Italian-Americans and,
        103-104, 105, 128, 139, 140-141
Crispino, James, xviii n, 128-130
*Cristiani*, 12
Cultural Center, Monte Carmelo, 26, 100

Day laborers, 1-2
Daycare center, 111
DeConde, A., xviii n
Democratic Club, 25, 29, 104
Democratic Party, 25, 98, 99
Depression, Great, 35, 53-54
DiDonato, Pietro, 101, 102

Disobedience, 49-50, *See also* Obedience
Disrespect, 6, 7, 49-50, 51

Education, 23, 35, 49, 53, 55, 56, 78,
    126. *See also* Schools, Catholic;
    Schools, public
    of females, 46, 78, 81, 86
    in southern Italy, 4, 8, 33, 66, 73,
        77, 82
Education, college, 23, 37, 42, 72, 74,
    83, 86
    of females, 55, 56, 66, 67, 75-76, 78,
        80, 84
Elderly, 31-33, 52-54
    housing for, 96
    Senior Citizens Association for, 25
Enclave, Monte Carmelo as Italian-
    American, 14, 21, 90, 119, 120,
        122, 123, 146
Enclavement process, 26-28, 40
Engagement, 85
English language, 43, 55, 76
    ethnic orientation and, 21, 23, 24, 48,
        71, 80
    ethnicity and, 130
English, Bella, 62 n
Envy, evil eye and, 11
Estate owners, 1, 2
Esthetics, 127
Ethclass, 135
Ethnic groups. *See also specific group*
    in Monte Carmelo, 26-27, 55, 87-91,
        119-120, 144
    in public schools, 36, 40, 49, 74, 75
Ethnic identity, 21, 24, 43, 54, 58,
    129-130
*Ethnic Myth: Race, Ethnicity, and Class in
    America, The* (Steinberg), 135
Ethnic orientation. *See also* Italian-
    Americans, in Monte Carmelo
    socio-cultural characteristics and, xvii,
        xviii, 21-24, 133-134
Ethnicity
    associations and, 131-133
    class and, xviii, 124-134, 135
    gender roles and, 131
    feasts and, 130-131
    food and, 130